The Meaning of
ENGLISH
Place Names

The Meaning of

ENGLISH
Place Names

EDWARD
HARRINGTON

THE
BLACKSTAFF
PRESS

First published in 1984
by The Blackstaff Press Limited
3 Galway Park, Dundonald, Belfast BT16 0AN

Photoset in 10 on 12 Sabon
by The Blackstaff Press
Printed in Northern Ireland by
The Universities Press Limited

British Library Cataloguing in Publication Data

Harrington, Edward
The meaning of English place names
1. Great Britain – Gazeteers
I. Title
914.1'00142   DA640

ISBN 0 85640 305 9

Cover photograph: Gold Hill, Shaftesbury, Dorset,
by Nicholas Servian/Woodmansterne.

Foreword

1. A WEALTH OF MEANINGS

Place names hold a wealth of meanings. They bear the traces of the main groups that colonised England (Celts, Romans, Anglo-Saxons, Scandinavians and Normans). They embody and recall history (Battle); they refer to old social orders (Knightsbridge and Carlton); and they retain pagan and Christian allusions (Harrow and Blackfriars). They include just about every kind of topography; roads (Holloway), river crossings (Oxford), valleys and fens (Sleddale and Marston), hills and ridges (Pendle and Ridgeway). They contain the names of ancestors, especially Anglo-Saxon ones who founded the earliest settlements of their peoples (Pevensey). They contain the names of all the trees that are indigenous to the country. They constitute the source of a great part of English surnames. To move around among these names and to have no idea of what they mean is to look and not see, to hear and not understand.

The dictionary section contains over 4,000 names. Given that many are found several times, it gives the meaning of over 10,000 English place names. Almost every village or town of over 4,000 inhabitants is included – and many more places besides. Places are located according to the new county boundaries. The old shires and counties were established in the eighth, ninth and tenth centuries when the place names were already old. The place names are, however, as likely to outlast the new administrative units as they have the old.

To give a little background to the dictionary, the next section sketches the impact of the main colonising groups on the names of places. Another section contains notes on the most common elements in names (-ton, -worth, -ham, -lea, -ing, -ing[ham]). At the back of the book there is to be found a glossary of root words. The glossary can be used as a 'do-it-yourself' kit for words that are not in the dictionary. But the reader needs to be warned that obvious etymology is often misleading. Where readers want to be sure of a meaning they must look up some of the standard books which are mentioned at the end of this foreword.

2. THE PEOPLES

(i) The Celts

The Celts (especially the Britons, who gave the whole island its name), are the oldest of the main colonising groups and settled here between 500 and 400 BC. They left behind names that are found most abundantly in the North and the West; and they gave names to many of the rivers. Celtic names are often found in higher, isolated spots that suggest that more remote groups remained Celtic-speaking long after other groups had accepted the language of the Anglo-Saxon conquerors. The often-recurring element Wal- originally referred to Celtic groups and continued to indicate Welsh settlements; later again it indicated serfs who did not have full civic rights.

(ii) The Romans

Though they came to England about 55 BC and controlled most of England for over three centuries, the Romans left only about 300 names behind. This small number suggests that Roman administrators used the existing Celtic names. The commonest Roman element – *ceaster, caester, chester* (Latin: *castra*) – is often added to a Celtic personal name or to a river name. Roman roads or streets provide a focus for the names given by later settlers (Stretton).

(iii) The Anglo-Saxons

The Angles, Saxons and Jutes arrived in the latter part of the fifth century. They gradually settled and took over England, giving most places their present names. The history of their settlement can in some measure be traced from the spread of the names they gave. Archaeology often combines fascinatingly with the study of place names to unravel the secrets of history. The oldest Anglo-Saxon elements – *-ham, -ing, -ton, -worth* – are settlement names. They combine with myriad other elements to create a wealth of references.

(iv) The Scandinavians

Towards the end of the ninth century, invaders from Scandinavia began to settle in England. They took over an area represented by modern Yorkshire, Derbyshire, Lincolnshire, Leicestershire, Norfolk and Suffolk. The area was called the Danelaw (that is, subject to Danish Law) and had been conquered by Danish groups. Other groups came from Norway (the latter came in part by way of Ireland – the placenames Aspatria and Ireton are examples of the legacy of the Irish Norwegians). The Scandinavians left a strong mark on the names of places that they founded or took over. *By*, which means 'farm' or 'village', is the commonest element, as in Derby, Formby, Whitby. *Thorp(e)* ('secondary settlement' or 'outlying farm') and *Thwaite* ('clearing') came from a period when the Danes had changed from being conquerors to being cultivators and traders who spread peacefully among their Anglo-Saxon neighbours as population numbers grew and uncultivated land was broken in.

(v) The Norman French

Like the Romans, the Normans left a small enough legacy of place names. It is true however that many French elements became incorporated into Middle English and are indistinguishable from it. A close correlation exists between the spread of French names and places where the Normans founded their castles and religious houses: castles like those at Richmond and Beaumont and religious houses like those at Haltemprice and Mount Grace. One interesting consequence of the Normans' use of language was to change pronunciations of existing names into sounds compatible with Norman-French. The Norman scribes (those of the Domesday book not least) changed spellings and pronunciations. The fashions set by the ruling groups explain other changes. The 'ch' sound of Old English, for example, tended to become 'c' sounded as 's': Gloucester, Leicester, Worcester. Similarly, the Old English 'g' before 'a' or 'e' changes into 'j': Jarrow, Jesmond.

3. COMMONEST OLD ENGLISH ELEMENTS

Ham

The oldest meaning of this word seems to have been 'farm', 'homestead' or 'estate'. It also designates a village. Later it came to denote a manor (Bispham). There is some evidence that in its earliest meanings it indicated a larger farm than *tun*. If it did, it is easier to understand the extension of meaning from an estate to the bigger building or manor that went with larger land holding. *Ham* is the ancestor of 'home' but in its earliest instances it is often hard to distinguish it from *hamm*, which usually means 'meadowland by a river'.

Leah

The earliest meaning was 'woodland'. Later it became 'clearing in woodland'. Thus its meaning tends to be 'woodland' or 'forest' in the oldest names and 'clearing' in later names. Mostly, however, it is impossible to know which meaning is indicated in a particular place. In any case both meanings go together, since a clearing implies woodland. It is associated especially with persons (Keighley) and trees (Purley). With time this element paradoxically came to designate open land – which was an extension of its meaning as clearing.

-ingas; -ingham; -ington

These constantly-found elements are difficult to interpret with full accuracy. They designate old settlements but probably not the oldest: *-ingas* is best rendered 'people of X' (personal name); *-ingham* 'settlement of X's followers'; and -*ington* 'farm or settlement associated with X's people'. The common element in these names is the reference to a founder (ancester hero) and/or his followers. In the dictionary I have tried to keep this reference but have not distinguished the various shades of meaning. Those who want to pursue the matter further should look up the discussion in Gelling's *Signposts to the Past*. There is a related -*ing* which is distinct. It is added to plants (Clavering) and other names (Bowling, Carling) and simply means 'place'.

Tun

This is the commonest element in place names. It goes right back to the earliest Anglo-Saxon settlements and means 'enclosure'. Since people built houses on their land, the meaning changed with time to 'homestead'. Since homesteads clustered, 'tun' came to mean a village – and thence on to become 'town' in modern English. Practically every other element ranging from names of persons and social groups to the names of rivers, trees and crops are compounded with '*tun*'.

4. FURTHER READING

The present little book is an introduction to meanings only. It depends on the scholarship of many studies. Those who want to pursue further an interest in place names need to move on to other works. The classic study is Eilert Ekwall, *English Place-Names* (Clarendon Press, 1960 edition). There is a good survey by William Addison, *Understanding*

English Place-Names (Batsford, 1978), that puts names in an historical context. John Field, *Place Names of Great Britain and Ireland* (David and Charles, 1980), provides a dictionary with neat historical notes added to meanings. Field also has a useful little introduction, *Discovering Place Names* (Shire Publications, 1978). There are two readable books by G. J. Copley, *Names and Places* (Phoenix House, 1963) and *English-Place Names and their Origins* (David and Charles, 1968). Kenneth Cameron, *English Place-Names* (Batsford, 1963 edition) combines scholarship and readability and can hardly be over-praised. For those who would venture a little further there is another scholarly study by Margaret Gelling, *Sign Posts to the Past* (Dent, 1978). Adrian Room's *Concise Dictionary of Modern Place Names in Great Britain and Ireland* (Oxford University Press, 1983) includes many names omitted from the standard sources, while A.L.F. Rivet and C. Smith's *Place Names of Roman Britain* (Batsford, 1979) is exhaustive on many of the more difficult names. Finally, for all who want to look up the place names of individual counties and to see accumulated and continuing scholarship the volumes of the English Place-Name Society survey are rich and indispensable.

The
Glossary

ABBREVIATIONS

Av	Avon	**L**	Lincolnshire
Bd	Bedfordshire	**La**	Lancashire
Bk	Buckinghamshire	**Le**	Leicestershire
Brk	Berkshire	**Lo**	London
Ca	Cambridgeshire	**Mr**	Merseyside
Ch	Cheshire	**Nb**	Northumberland
Cle	Cleveland	**Nf**	Norfolk
Co	Cornwall	**Nt**	Nottinghamshire
Cu	Cumbria	**Nth**	Northamptonshire
D	Devon	**O**	Oxfordshire
Db	Derbyshire	**Sa**	Shropshire
Do	Dorset	**Sf**	Suffolk
Du	Durham	**So**	Somerset
ES	East Sussex	**Sr**	Surrey
Ess	Essex	**St**	Staffordshire
Gl	Gloucestershire	**T & W**	Tyne and Wear
GM	Greater Manchester	**W**	Wiltshire
		Wa	Warwickshire
Ha	Hampshire	**WM**	West Midlands
H & W	Hereford and Worcester	**WS**	West Sussex
		YN	North Yorkshire
Hm	Humberside	**YS**	South Yorkshire
Hrt	Hertfordshire	**YW**	West Yorkshire
IW	Isle of Wight		
K	Kent		

Abberton (Ess): Eadburg's (a woman's name) farm or enclosure.

Abbey Dore (H & W): Abbey on the (river) Dore ('Dore' is from a Celtic word meaning 'river' or 'stream').

Abbotsbury (Do): Abbot's manor.

Abingdon (O): Aebba's hill.

Abinger (Sr): Enclosure of Eabba's people.

Abloads (Gl): Abba's ferry.

Abram (GM): Eadburg's (a woman's name) homestead.

Acaster Malbis (YW): Roman fort at the river (belonging to the Malbis family).

Acaster Selby (YW): Roman fort at the river (belonging to Selby Abbey).

Accrington (La): Acorn farm or enclosure.

Acklam (Cle, YN): ?(Place) at the oak woods; ?(Place on) slopes.

Ackroyd (YW): Clearing among oaks.

Ackworth (YW): Acca's enclosure.

Acle (Nf): Oak wood.

Acomb (Nb, YN, YW): Place of oak trees.

Acre (La , Nf): Plot of arable land.

Acton (common): Oak farm or enclosure.

Acton (Nb, Sf): Acca's enclosure or farm.

Adber (Do): Eata's grove.

Adderbury (O): Eadburg's (a woman's name) fort.

Addingham (Cu, YW): Place of Adda's people.

Addington (Bk, Co, K, Lo, Nth): Farm or enclosure of Eadda's people.

Addiscombe (Lo): Eadda's enclosed piece of land.

Addlestone (Sr): Attel's valley.

Adel (YW): Dirty place.

Adlington (Ch, La): Farm or enclosure of Eadwulf's people.

Adwick (YS): Adda's dwelling or farm (outlying farm).

Aigburth (Mr): Oak hill.

Aintree (Mr): Single tree.

Aire (River) (Yorks & Hm): Strong river.

Aiskew (YN): Oak wood.

Akeley (Bk): Oak wood.

Albury (Hrt, O, Sr): Old fort.

Alcester, Alchester (O, Wa, WM): Roman fort on the (river) Alne ('bright').

Aldborough (Nf, YN, YW): Old fort.

Aldborough Hatch (La): (Place at) the forest gate of the Albourgh family.

Aldbury (Nf, YN, YW): Old fort.

Aldeburgh (Sf): Old fort.

Aldenham (Hrt): Old homestead.

Alderley (Ch): Ealdred's wood.

Alderley (Gl): Alder wood.

Aldermaston (Brk): Nobleman's farm or manor.

Alderminster (Wa): Nobleman's farm or manor.

Aldersbrook (Lo): Alder stream.

Aldersey (Ch): Aldhere's river land.

Aldershaw (St): Alder copse.

Aldershot (Ha): Corner of land with alder trees.

Alderton (Gl, Nth, Sf, W): Ealdhere's farm or enclosure.

Alderton (Sa): Alder-tree farm or enclosure.

Aldgate (Lo): Ale gate.

Aldridge (WM): Building by the alder trees.

Aldwych (Lo): Old farm.

Alford (So): Old ford.

Alford (L): Alder ford.

Alfreton (Db): Aelfred's farm or enclosure.

Alfriston (ES): Aelfric's farm or enclosure.

Alkham (K): Homestead by the (pagan) temple.

Allerdale (Cu): ?Valley of the (river) Alen; ?White river.

Allerton (Mr, YW, YN): Alder farm.

Allonby (Cu): Alein's village or farm.

Almondbury (YW): Fort of all the men, fort belonging to everybody (communal property).

Alne (River) (YN): White river or bright river.

Alnwick (Nb): Dwelling or building on the (river) Aln; ?Holy or strong river; ?White river.

Alresford (Ess) (same as **Aylesford**): Aegel's ford.

Alresford (Ha): Alder tree ford.

Alrewas (St): Alder swamp.

Alsager (Ch): Aelle's field.

Alsop (Db): Aelle's little valley.

Alston (Cu): Aldhun's farm or enclosure.

Alston (D): Alwine's farm or enclosure.

Althorp (Nth): Olla's outlying village or farm.

Alton (Db, Le): Old farm.

Alton (Do, Ha): Spring farm; Farm at the source of a river.

Alton (St): Aelfa's farm.

Altrincham (GM): Homestead of Aldhere's people.

Alvechurch (H & W): Aelfgyth's (a woman's name) church.

Alverstoke (Ha): Aelfweard's or Aethelweard's outlying farm.

Alwoodley (YW): Aethelwald's wood or clearing.

Amber (Db): River or water.

Amble (Nb): Anna's (a man's name) headland.

Amblecote (WM): Aemela's (?) cottage.

Ambleside (Cu): Shieling (summer or temporary dwelling) by a river sandbank.

Amersham (Bk): Ealhmund's homestead.

Amesbury (W): Ambr's fort.

Ampleforth (YN): Sorrel ford.

Ampthill (Bd): ?Ant heap; ?Hill abounding in ants.

Ancoats (La): Lonely or isolated cottage.

Andover (Ha): River or water (place).

Anglezark (La): Anlaf's shieling.

Angmering (WS): (Place of) Angenmaer's people.

Angram (YN): Pasture lands.

Anst(e)y (common): Narrow (single-file) path.

Apperley (G1, YW): Apple-tree wood or clearing.

Appleby (common): Farmstead or village where apples grow.

Appledore (Co): Ford by an apple tree.

Appledore (D, K): (Place of) apple trees.

Applegarth (YN): Apple orchard.

Appleton (common): Apple orchard; apple farm.

Ap(p)ley (common): Apple-tree wood or clearing.

Apsley (common): Aspen wood.

Arbury (common): Earthwork fort.

Arden (Ch, K, Hm): Dwelling house.

Arden (Wa): High place.

Arden (YN): ?Eagle valley; ?Gravel valley.

4

Ardingley (WS): Wood or clearing of Earda's or Eored's people.

Ardwick (GM): Aethelred's dwelling or building.

Ar(e)ley (common): Eagle wood.

Argam (Hm): Shieling, hill or summer pasture place.

Arkengarthdale (YN): Dale of Arnkell's enclosure.

Arkholme (La): (Place) at the hill pastures.

Arleston (Db): Earl's farm.

Arleston (Sa): Eardwulf's farm or enclosure.

Arley (common): Eagle wood or clearing.

Arlington (D): Farm or enclosure of Aelfrith's people.

Armley (YW): Wretched or poor wood.

Arne (Do): House.

Arn(e)cliff(e) (YN, YW): Eagle cliff.

Arnos Grove (Lo): Small wood belonging to the Arnold family.

Arnside (Cu): Earnwulf's headland.

Arnwood (Ha): Eagle wood.

Array (Hm): Place of summer pasture, shielings.

Arrowfield (H & W): Open country with a (pagan) shrine.

Arun (river) (WS): Named from **Arundel**.

Arundel (WS): Hoarhound valley.

Asby (common): See **Ashby**.

Ascot (Brk, O): Eastern cottage(s).

Ash (common): (Place by) ash trees.

Ashbourne (Db): Ash tree stream.

Ashburton (D): Farmstead alongside the ash-tree stream.

Ashby (common): Farmstead or village where ash trees abound.

Ashdown (ES, O): Hill country with ash trees.

Ashdown (Brk): Aesc's hill.

Ash(e) (common): (Place by) ash trees.

Ashford (D, DB, K, Sa): Ash-tree ford.

Ashford (Lo): ?Ford by the church; ?Ford by oak trees.

Ashington (Nb): Valley with ash trees.

Ashington (So): (Place in) the east of the village.

Ashley (common): Ash-tree wood.

Ashover (Db): Ash-tree slope.

Ashridge (Hrt): Ridge with ash trees.

Ashtead (Sr): Place of ash trees.

Ashton (common): Ash-tree farm or enclosure.

Ashurst (common): Ash-tree wood or wooded hill.

Ashwood (common): Ash-tree wood.

Aske (YN): Place of ash trees.

Askern (YS): ?House by ash trees; ?Ash-tree nook.

Askham (Cu, YN): Ash-tree homestead.

Askwith (YW): Ash wood.

Aspatria (Cu): Patrick's (Irish–Norwegian name) ash tree.

Aspley (Bd, Nt, St, Wa): Aspen wood.

Aspull (GM): Aspen hill.

Astcot(s) (common): Eastern cottages.

Astley (common): Eastern wood or clearing.

Aston (common): Usually this name means 'eastern farmstead' or 'village'; sometimes it means 'ash-tree farm'.

Atcham (Sa): Homestead of Aetti's or Eata's people.

Athelney (So): Island of the princes.

Atherstone (So, Wa): Eadric's farm or enclosure.

Atherton (GM): Aethelhere's farm or enclosure.

Attercliffe (YS): (Place) at the cliff or steep slope.

Attingham (Sa): See **Atcham**.

Attleborough (Nf, Wa): Aetla's fort.

Auburn (Hm): Eel stream.

Auckland (Du): Cliff at the rock on the Clyde (?clear river); Land held by the Bishop of Durham.

Audenshaw (GM): Aldwine's copse.

Audlem (Ch): Old Lyme or part of Lyme, belonging to Alda (Alda's Lyme). (Lyme is derived from 'elm'.)

Audley (St): Aldgyth's (a woman's name) wood or clearing.

Aughton (La, YS, W): Oak farm or enclosure.

Austerfield (YS): Sheepfold in open country.

Austwick (YN): East village.

Avebury (W): Affa's fort.

Aveley (Ess): Aelfgyth's (a woman's name) forest or clearing.

Avon (river) (common): River (a Celtic name).

Axe (river) (D, Do, So): Water (a Celtic name).

Axholme (Hm): Holme or island belonging to Haxey (Haxey is 'Hakr's island').

Axminster (D): Religious foundation on the (river) Axe.

Aylesbury (Bk): Aegel's fort.

Aylesford (K): Aegel's ford.

Aylsham (Nf): Aegel's homestead.

Aymot (YN): Confluence of waters.

Aynho (Nth): Aega's spur of land.

Aysgarth (YN): Pass of the oak wood.

Ayston (Le): Aethelstan's farm or enclosure.

Ayton (YN): Farm on a river.

Babbacome (D): Babba's valley.

Baber (Lo): Babba's enclosure.

Babergh (Sf): ?Babba's fort or mound.

Backworth (T & W): Bacca's enclosure.

Bacton (H & W, Nf, Sf): Bacca's farm.

Bacup (La): Small valley by a ridge.

Badeworth (Gl, So): Baegga's enclosure.

Badminton (Av): Farm of Beadumund's people.

Bagley (Brk, Sa, So, YW): ?Badger wood.

Bagshaw (Db): ?Badger copse.

Bagshot (Sr, W): ?Corner of land with badgers.

Bagslate (La): Bacga's valley.

Bagworth (Le): Bacga's enclosure.

Baildon (YW): ?Curved hill; ?Berry hill.

Bakewell (Db): Badeca's spring.

Baldock (Hrt): 'Baldoc' is Old French for 'Baghdad'. The name was given by the Knights Templar.

Balham (Lo): ?Bealga's river meadow; ?Round river meadow.

Balsall (WM): Baelli's corner of land.

Bamber (La): ?Bimme's bridge.

Bamburgh (Nb): Bebbe's fort.

Bampton (Cu, O): Farm dwelling made of beams.

Bampton (D): Farm of those who live near a bath or hot spring.

Banbury (O): Bana's fort

Banham (Nf): Homestead where beans are grown.

Bank(s) (common): Hill slope, bank, ridge.

Bankend (Cu): ?Bottom of a hill.

Bank Head (Db, Nb): ?Head of the ridge or hill slope.

Bank Newton (Hm): Hillside belonging to the Newtons.

Bankside (Lo, YS): Side of a hill.
Bannawell (Lo): Well or spring of the slayer.
Banstead (Sr): Place where beans are grown.
Banwell (Av): Well or spring of the slayer.
Bapchild (K): Bacca's cold spring.
Barbican (D, Lo): Strongly fortified gate, outer fortification.
Barbourne (H & W): Beaver stream.
Barbury (W): Bera's fort.
Barden (YN, YW): Barley valley.
Bare (La): Grove.
Barford (**Barforth**) (common): Barley ford.
Barham (Ca, Sf): Hill homestead.
Barham (K): Biora's homestead.
Bark(e)ston(e) (Le, L, YN): Borkr's farm or enclosure.
Barking (Lo, Sf): (Place of) Berica's people.
Barley (common): Usually it means 'clearing where barley is grown'; sometimes it means 'boar wood'.
Barlinch (So): Bank where barley grows.
Barling(s) (Ess, L): (Place of) Baerla's people.
Barlow (Db): ?Boar wood; ?Clearing where barley is grown.
Barlow (La): Barley hill.
Barlow (YN): ?Hill with a barn; ?Barley hill.
Barnack (Nth): ?Beorn's building or settlement.
Barnes (Lo): Barns.
Barnet (Hrt, Lo): Place cleared by burning.
Barnetby le Wold (Hm): Beornoth's village (the wood).
Barnham (Nf, Sf, WS): Beorna's homestead.
Barnoldswick (La): Beornwulf's village or settlement

Barnsley (YS): Beorn's wood or clearing.

Barnstaple (D): ?Bearda's staple or post; ?Post with a beard (a marker of sorts).

Barnwell (Ca): Beorn's spring.

Barnwell (Nth): Stream by the burial mound.

Barrow (common): Three main meanings: 1, (Place) at the grove or wood; 2, Hill; 3, Tumulus or burial mound.

Barrow (Sf, So): Hill or burial mound.

Barrow-in-Furness (Cu): Hilly island (see **Furness**).

Barrowford (La): Wood ford.

Barsham (Nf, Sf): ?Bar's homestead; ?Boar homestead.

Barton (common): Two main meanings: 1, Barley farm; 2, Outlying grange for storing crops.

Barwick (Hrt, Nf, So, YW): Barley farm.

Basford (Ch, St): ?Beorcol's ford; Birch ford.

Basford (Nt): Basa's ford.

Basildon (Ess): Beorhtel's hill.

Basingstoke (Ha): Farm or outlying settlement belonging to Basa's people.

Bassenthwaite (Cu): Bastun's clearing.

Bassetlawe (Nt): Hill of the dwellers in land cleared by burning.

Bath (Av): (Roman) baths.

Batley (YW): Bata's wood or clearing.

Battersea (Lo): Beaduric's island.

Battle (ES): (Site of the) battle (of Hastings).

Bawtry (YS): Balda's tree.

Baxterley (Wa): Wood or clearing of the baker.

Bayswater (Lo): ?Bayard's watering place.

Beachy Head (ES): Beautiful headland.
Beacon Hill (common): A hill on which a beacon or warning fire is lit.
Beaconsfield (Bk): Open land with a beacon.
Beaminster (Do): Religious foundation or church of Bebbe or her people.
Beamish (Du): Beautiful mansion.
Beaulieu (Ha): Beautiful place.
Beaumont (common): Beautiful hill.
Beauworth (Ha): Bee enclosure.
Bebington (Mr): Bebbe's farm or enclosure.
Beccles (Sf): Stream pasture.
Beckenham (Lo): Beohha's homestead.
Beckery (So): Little Ireland.
Beckett (Nf): Bee hut or cottage.
Beckingham (L, Nt): Homestead of Becca's people.
Beckington (So): Homestead of Becca's people.
Beckwith (YN): Beech wood.
Becontree (Lo): Beohha's tree.
Bedale (YN): Beda's corner of land.
Beddington (Lo): Beada's farm or enclosure.
Bedfont (Lo): ?Spring led into a trough (to make drawing water easier); ?Spring in a hollow.
Bedford (Bd, Lo): Beda's ford.
Bedlington (Nb): Enclosure of Bedla's people.
Bedwell (Hrt): Spring in a valley.
Bedworth (Wa): Beda's enclosure.
Beer (D, Do, So): Grove; Woodland pasture.
Be(e)sthorpe (L, Nf, Nt): Outlying farm where sedge grows.
Beeston (Nf, Nt, St, YW): Sedge or bent-grass farm.

Belaugh (Nf): Funeral pyre enclosure.

Belford (Nb): (Unexplained element) ford.

Belgrave (St): ?Grove near which funeral pyres are made; ?Beautiful grove.

Bellasize (Hm): Well situated.

Bellingham (Lo, Nb): (Place of) Beora's people.

Belmont (Lo): Beautiful hill.

Belper (Db): Beautiful retreat.

Belsize (Lo): Well situated.

Belstead (Ess, Sf): Place of funeral pyres.

Beltoft (Hm): Cremation plot.

Belton (Hm, L, Le): Enclosure for funeral pyres.

Belvedere (common): Fine view.

Belvoir (Le): Beautiful view.

Bembridge (W): Inside the bridge.

Bemersley (St): Clearing or wood of the trumpeter.

Bemerton (W): Farm of the trumpeter.

Benacre (Sf): Plot of arable land in which beans are grown.

Benenden (K): Woodland or swine pasture of Bionna's people.

Benfleet (Ess): Tree-trunk creek (referring to a bridge).

Benhilton (Lo): Farm at the hill on which beans are grown.

Bensham (Du): Cattle shelter on a bank.

Bentham (Gl, YN): Homestead in a place where bent grass (a coarse grass) grows.

Bentley (common): Clearing where bent grass grows.

Benwell (T & W): (Place) within the (Roman) wall.

Beoley (H & W): Bee clearing.

Bere (D, Do): Grove.

Berechurch (Ess): Timber church (made of planks).

Bere Regis (Do): Wood of the king.

Berk(e)ley (Gl, So): Birch wood.

Berkhamsted (Hrt): ?Birch-tree homestead; ?Homestead by a hill.

Berkshire: Hill shire.

Bermondsey (Lo): Beornmund's marshy land or island.

Berwick (common): Barley farm.

Besthorpe: See **Beesthorpe**.

Bethnal (Green) (Lo): Blitha's corner of land (village green).

Betteshanger (K): Building by a hanging or steep wood.

Bevercotes (Nt): Huts near where beavers are found.

Beverley (Hm, Lo, YW): Beaver stream.

Beversbrook (W): Beaver brook.

Bew(d)ley (Cu, H & W): Beautiful place.

Bewick (Nb, YE): Bee farm.

Bexhill (ES): Box-tree wood.

Bexley (Lo): Box-tree wood.

Bibury (Gl): Beage's fort.

Bicester (O): ?Beorna's Roman fort; ?Roman fort of the warriors; ?Roman fort of the burial ground.

Bickershaw (GM): Beekeepers' copse.

Bickerstaffe (La): Landing place of the beekeepers.

Bickerton (common): Beekeepers' farm.

Bicknor (K): Bica's slope.

Bicknor (H & W): Bica's ridge.

13

Biddenden

Biddenden (K): Bida's swine pasture.

Biddulph (St): Place alongside a quarry.

Bideford (D): Byda's ford.

Bidwell (common): Spring in a valley.

Biggin(s) (common): Buildings, outhouses, dwellings.

Biggleswade (Bd): Biccel's ford.

Bildeston (Sf): Bild's farm or enclosure.

Billericay (Ess, K): Meaning is unexplained.

Billing (Nth): (Place of) Billa's people.

Billinge (Mr): Hill.

Billingham (Cle, IW): Homestead of Billa's people.

Billingsgate (Lo): Landing place belonging to Billing.

Billingshurst (WS): Wooded hill of Billa's people.

Bilston (Hm, Nb, YN): Billa's farm.

Bilton (Wa): ?Henbane farm.

Bingham (Nt): ?Homestead in a hollow; ?Homestead of Bynna's people.

Bingley (YW): Wood or clearing of Bynna's people.

Birchill(s) (Db, St): Birch hill.

Birchover (Db): Riverbank abounding in birches.

Birdbrook (Ess): Bird brook.

Birdham (WS): Enclosure frequented by birds.

Birdlip (Gl): ?Bird slope; Bride's leap.

Birkdale (Mr, YN): Birch-tree valley.

Birkenhead (Mr): Birch headland.

Birkenshaw (YW): Birch copse.

Birkenside (Nb): Hillside abounding in birches.

Birker (Cu): Hill pasture, shieling among birch trees.

Birley (Db, H & W, YS): Forest clearing with a byre.

Birling (ES, K, Nb): (Place of) Baerla's people.

Birmingham (WM): Homestead of Beorma's people.
Birstal(l) (Le, YW): Old fort.
Birtley (Nb, T & W): Bright wood or clearing.
Bishopsteignton (D): Farm on the (river) Teign held by the Bishop (of Exeter).
Bishopston(e) (common): Bishop's farm (from which the bishop draws the revenue).
Bispham (La): Bishop's house.
Bix (O): (Place of) box trees.
Blaby (Le): ?Village of the dark man; ?Bla's village.
Blackburn (La, Nt, YS): Dark stream.
Blackford (common): Black ford.
Blackfriars (Lo, O): (Priory of the) black brothers or Dominicans.
Blackpool (La): Dark pool.
Blackrod (GM): Dark clearing.
Blackeney (Gl, Nf): ?Black island; ?Blaca's island.
Blanchland (Nb): White clearing.
Blandford (Do): Gudgeon ford.
Blaydon (T & W): Dark hill.
Bletchley (Bk, Sa): Blecca's wood or clearing.
Blidworth (Nth): Blithe's enclosure.
Blindwell (common): Hidden or concealed well.
Bloomsbury (Lo): Manor of the de Blemunds.
Bluntisham (Ca): Blunt's homestead.
Blyth(e) (common): Gentle river.
Blythburgh (Sf): Fort on the (river) Blythe.
Boarhunt (Ha): Spring near a fort.
Bodmin (Co): ?House or hut of the monks.
Bognor (WS): Bucge's (a woman's name) foreshore.
Bold (Mr, Sa): Place where buildings stand, dwelling.

Boldon (T & W, Sa): ?Rounded hill; ?Hill with a dwelling.

Bollington (Ch): Farm by the (river) Bolling.

Bolsover (Db): ?Bol's slope; ?Bullock pasture.

Bolton (common): Enclosure with buildings, collection of buildings, main village.

Bonchurch (IW): ?Church of the slayer; ?Buna's church.

Bondgate (common): Street of the bondsmen or unfree tenants.

Bond Street (common): Street of the unfree tenants.

Bookham (Sr): Birch enclosure or homestead.

Booth (YW): Booth(s), temporary shelters.

Bootham Bar (York): Gate at the booths or stalls.

Boothferry (Hm): Ferry by Booth.

Bootle (Cu, La): Dwelling place.

Bordesley (H & W, WM): ?Brord's wood or clearing.

Bordon (Ha): ?Swine pasture.

Borough (Lo): Fort, fortified place.

Boroughbridge (YN): Bridge by the fort.

Borrowash (Db): Ash tree by the fort.

Borrowdale (Cu): Valley of the fort.

Borstal (K): Place of refuge.

Borwick (La): Outlying part of an estate.

Boscastle (Co): De Botereus' castle.

Bostall (Lo): Same as **Borstal**.

Boston (L): (St?) Botulf's stone (i.e., church built in stone).

Bosworth (Le): Bar's enclosure or farm.

Botolph Lane (Lo): Lane of the church of St Botolph.

Bottesford (Hm, Le): Ford by or belonging to a house.

Bottom, Bothom (common): Valley bottom.

Boughton (common): ?Beech farm; ?Farm held by a charter.

Boughton (L, Nf, Nt, Nth): ?Buck-goat farm; ?Bucca's farm.

Bourn(e) (common): (Place by) a spring or stream.

Bournemouth (Ha): Mouth of the stream.

B(o)urton (common): Farm or settlement by a fort.

Bovey Tracey (D): Place on the (river) Bovey held by de Tracy.

Bovington (Do): Farm or enclosure of Bofa's people.

Bow (Cu, D, Lo, YW): Arch (or a bridge).

Bowburn (Du): Curving stream.

Bowdon, Bowden (Ch, Db, Du, Le): Curved hill.

Bowes (YN): Curving stream.

Bowland (La, YW): Land alongside a river bend.

Bowling (YW): A bowl-shaped hollow.

Bowness (Cu): ?Bull headland; ?Bow-shaped headland.

Box (Gl, Hrt, W): (Place of) box trees.

Boxcombe (Do, W): Box-tree valley.

Boxford (Brk, Sf): Box-tree ford.

Boxgrove (WS): Box-tree grove.

Box Hill (Sr): Box-tree hill.

Boxley (K): Box-tree wood.

Boycott (Bk, Sa ,H & W): ?Hut of the servant; ?Boia's hut.

Boynton (Hm): Farm or enclosure of Bofa's people.

Boythorpe (Db, Hm): ?Small settlement of servants; ?Boia's village.

17

Boyton (common): ?Servants' farm; ?Boia's farm.

Bracken (Hu): Place where ferns or bracken abound.

Brackenthwaite (Cu, YN): Fern clearing.

Brackley (Brk, Db, Nth): Bracken wood or clearing.

Bracknell (Brk): ?Nook of land where bracken grows; ?Bracca's nook of land.

Bradenham(s) (Bk, Nf): Broad or wide river meadow; Wide homestead.

Bradfield (common): Spacious tract of open country.

Bradford (common): Broad or wide ford.

Brading (IW): (Place of the) border people.

Bradley (common): Broad or wide wood or clearing.

Bradshaw (Db, La, YW): Large wood.

Bradwell (common): Wide stream.

Bradworthy (D): Broad or wide enclosure.

Brailsford (Db): Ford by the burial place.

Braintree (Ess): Bran(u)ca's(?) tree.

Braithwaite (Cu, YN, YS, YW): Broad clearing in a wood.

Bramber (WS): Bramble thicket.

Bramham (YW): Homestead with broom.

Bramhope (YW): Small, enclosed valley in which broom grows.

Bramley (common): Broom thicket.

Brampton (common): Broom farm.

Bramshaw (Ha): Bramble copse.

Brancepeth (Du): ?Path to Brandon.

Bran(d)t (L, Nt, Nth): Clearing created by burning.

Brandon (common): Broom hill.

Brandred (K): Clearing made by burning.

Brandwood (La, WM): Wood cleared by burning.

Brant Broughton (L): Brook village or fortified manor destroyed by fire.

Bratton (common): Farm of land newly broken-in for cultivating.

Braunston (Le, Nth): Brand's farm or enclosure.

Braunton (D): Broom farm.

Braxted (Ess): Place abounding in bracken.

Bray (Brk, D): Hill brow, hill.

Breach (common): Newly broken-in land.

Breamore (Ha): Moor abounding in broom.

Breaston (Db): Braegd's farm or enclosure.

Breckland (Nf): Newly cleared land.

Bredbury (Ch): Fort constructed with planks.

Bredgar (K): Broad triangular plot of land.

Bredwardine (H & W): Hillside enclosure or farm.

Bre(e)don (H & W, Le): Hill (both elements mean 'hill').

Breeches (K): Newly broken-in land.

Breedsall (Db): ?Nook on a hill.

Brendon (D): Brown hill(s).

Brent (Lo): High or holy river.

Brentford (Lo): Ford on the (river) Brent.

Brent Pelham (Hrt): Burnt Pelham ('Pelham' means 'Peola's homestead').

Brentwood (Ess): Burnt wood.

Brereton (Ch): ?Enclosure made by planting briars; ?Briar farm.

Brewood (St): Wood on a hill.

Brid(e)well (D, W): Well or spring of the bride.

Bridgemere (Ch): Bird water or pool.

Bridgend (common): Part of town or village at the bridge.

Bridgford (Nt): Ford over which a bridge has been built.

Bridgnorth (Sa): Northern bridge.

Bridgwater (So): Bridge in Walter's (de Douai) manor.

Bridlington (Hm): Farm of Beorhtel's people.

Bridport (Do): Market town attached to the manor of Bredy.

Brierley (common): Clearing in which briars grow.

Brigg (Hm): Bridge.

Briggate (Nf, YW): Bridge Street.

Brighouse (YW): Houses at the bridge.

Brightlingsea (Ess): Brihtric's island.

Brighton (ES): Beorhthelm's farm or enclosure.

Brightside (YS): Bric's ploughed land.

Brill (Bk, Lo): Hill.

Brind (Hm): Clearing made by burning, burnt place.

Brindley (La, St, YN): Clearing made by burning.

Briscoe (D, YN): Wood of the Britons.

Brislington (Av): Beorhthelm's farm.

Bristol (Av): Gathering-place at a bridge.

Britain: Land of the Britons ('tattooed people').

Britford (W): Bride's spring.

Brixham (D): Beorhtsige's or Brioc's homestead.

Brixton (Lo): Beorhstige's or Brioc's stone.

Brixton (D): Beorhtric's enclosure or farm.

Brixworth (Nth): Beorhtel's enclosure.

Broadcarr (Nf): Broad marsh.

Broadclyst (D): Broad place on the (river) Clyst.

Broadfield (common): Wide, extensive, open country.

Broadstairs (K): Wide steps (to the sea).

Broadwas (H & W): Broad or extensive marsh.

Broadwater (common): Wide stream.

Broadway (common): Wide road or street.

Broadwell (Gl, O, Sf, Wa): Broad spring.

Brockdish (Nf): Enclosed pasture or park with a stream.

Brockhall (Nth): Badger hole.

Brockham (Sr): ?Badger homestead; ?Village with a brook; ?Broc's homestead.

Brockenhurst (Ha): Broca's wood.

Brockhurst (Ha): Badger wood.

Brockley (Av, Lo, Sf): ?Wood or clearing with a stream; ?Broca's wood or clearing.

Brocton (Sa): Brook farm.

Bromley (common): Broom thicket.

Brompton (common): Broom farm.

Bromsgrove (H & W): Breme's grove.

Bromyard (H & W): Broom enclosure.

Bro(o)me (common): Place where broom is abundant.

Bro(o)mfield (common): Open country where broom is abundant.

Broomhill (common): Hill on which broom grows abundantly.

Broomhill (ES): Plum (tree) hill.

Brough (common): Fort, fortified place.

Brougham (Cu): ?Badger place; ?Heather place; ?Homestead by a fort.

Broughton (common): Three main meanings:

1, Farm on or by a brook; 2, Farm by a fort; 3, Farm by a hill or barrow.

Brownrigg (Cu): Hill brow.

Brownsea (Do): Brun's island.

Brownside (common): Brown hillside.

Broxbourne (Hrt): Badger stream.

Broxtowe (Nt): Brocwulf's place.

Bruton (So): Farm on the (river) Brue.

Buckden (Ca, YN): Valley of the buck deer.

Buckfast (D): Stronghold of the buck or male deer.

Buckfastleigh (D): The wood of the Buckfast.

Buckholt (Gl, Ha, K): Beech wood.

Buckhurst (Ess, K): Beech wood.

Buckingham (Bk): Enclosure of Bucc's people.

Buckland (common): Book land (i.e., land granted by royal charter).

Buckley (D, GM, Mr, Wa): Bullock clearing.

Buckton (GM, H & W, Hm, Nb): Deer enclosure or farm.

Buckworthy (D): Bullock enclosure.

Budbridge (IW): ?Bridge of logs; ?Bota's bridge.

Bud(d)le (Ha, IW, Nb): Buildings.

Bude (Co): ?(Place on the) rough river.

Budleigh (D): Budda's wood or clearing (see 'Salterton').

Buildwas (Sa): Building in a wet or marshy place.

Bulcamp (Sf): Bull or bullock enclosure.

Bulkington (W, Wa): Farm or enclosure of Bulca's people.

Bullingdon (O): ?Bula's hill; ?Bull's hill.

Bullring (common): Ring or enclosure for bull-baiting.

Bulmer (Ess, YN): Bull lake.

Bulwick (Nth): Bull farm.

Bumpstead (Ess): ?Buna's place; ?Place of reeds.

Bungay (Sf): Island of Buna's people.

Bunhill (Lo): Place by bone heaps.

Bunny (Nt): Reed island.

Buntingford (Hrt): ?Ford of Bunta's people; ?Bunting (a small bird) island.

Bunwell (Nf): Spring with reeds.

Burcot(t) (common): Cottages, dwellings.

Bures (Ess, Sf): Cottages, dwellings.

Burford (O, Sa, So): Ford by a fort.

Burgate (Ha, Sf, Sr): Gate of a fort.

Burgh (common): Fortified place, manor house.

Burley (common): Wood by a fort.

Burmarsh (K): Marsh of the Burhware (Canterbury people).

Burnett (Av): Burnt place (place cleared by burning).

Burnham (common): Two main meanings: 1, Meadow by the stream; 2, Homestead by the stream.

Burnley (La): Forest or clearing by the (river) Brun ('brown one').

Burnsall (YW): Bryni's corner of land.

Burnt Butts (YE): Place of burned tree-stumps.

Burntwood (St): Burned wood.

Burroughs (Lo): Place on a hill.

Burscough (La): Wood by the fort.

Burslem (St): Burgheard's (?) forest.

Burwash (ES): Tillage by a fort.

Burwell (Ca): Spring by a fort.

Burton (common): Farmstead or settlement near a fort.

Bury (GM): (Place) at the fort.

Buscot (O): Burgweard's cot or hut.

Bushey (Hrt): Enclosure by a thicket.

Buttermere (Cu): Lake by pastures good for butter.

Buttertubs (YW): Butter valley.

Butterwick (common): Butter, dairy farm.

Butterworth (La, YW): Butter enclosure.

Buxton (Db, Nf): ?Rocking stone; ?Bucc's stone; ?Buck's stone.

Bywell (Nb): Spring in the river bend.

Cadbury (D, So): Cada's fort.

Caister (Nf): Roman fort.

Caistor (L): Roman fort.

Calcot (Bd, Brk, Sa): Cold cottage (in a bleak place?); Shelter for travellers.

Caldbeck (Cu): Cold spring.

Caldecot(e)(s) (common): Cold cottage(s) or hut(s); Shelter(s) for travellers.

Calder (river) (Cu, La, YW): Rapid or rough stream.

Caldicote (H & W): See **Caldecot**.

Callington (Co): Farm by a forest.

Calne (W): ?Noisy river.

Calton (Db, St): Calf (-rearing) farm.

Calverley (YW): Clearing of the calves.

Calverton (Bk, Nt): Calf (-rearing) farm.

Cam (Gl): Crooked.

Cambeck (Cu): Crooked beck or stream.

Camberley (Sr): This place was called Cambridge Town in 1862 after the Duke of Cambridge. In 1877 it was changed to the present name because it tended to get mixed up with Cambridge.

Camberwell (Lo): 'Well' is 'spring'; 'Camber' may mean 'crane', but the meaning is unsure.

Camborne (Co): Crooked hill.

Cambridge: Bridge on the Granta ('fen river').

Camden (Lo): A name taken from Earl Camden, a large property-owner in the area.

Cameley (Av): Forest on the (river) Cameler ('crooked river').

Camelford (Co): Ford on the crooked river.

Campden (Gl): Valley with an enclosed field.

Candover (Ha): Fine or pleasant stream.

Cannock (St): Hill.

Cannon Hill (Lo): Hill of the canons (of Merton Priory).

Canonbury (Lo): Manor of the canons (of St Bartholomew's, Smithfield).

Canterbury (K): City of the Cantware (Kent dwellers).

Canvey (Ess): Island of Cana's people.

Capel (common): (Place with) a chapel.

Capel Craig (Cu): Horse rock.

Capernwray (La): Chapman's valley.

Caplerigg (Cu): Horse ridge.

Caradoc (H & W): Caradoc's fort.

Caradon (Co): Hill (both elements have the same meaning).

Carden (Ch): ?Enclosure with a cairn; ?Rock enclosure.

Cardew (Cu): Black fort.

Cardington (Bd): Farm associated with or belonging to Cenred.

Carham (Nb): (Place) at the rocks.

Carhampton (So): (Place) at the rocks ('ton' was added later).

Cark (La): Rock.

Carl(e)ton (common): Farm or enclosure of the free peasants.

Carlisle (Cu): Town of Luguvalos (a British personal name).

Carnforth (La): Crane ford.

Carrick (Co): Rock.

Carshalton (Lo): Cress-spring farm.

Carswell (Brk): Cress spring.

Cartmel (Cu): Sandbank by a rocky place.

Cassington (O): Cress farm.

Castle Carrock (Cu): Fortified castle.

Castleton (Db, Do, GM, YN): Farm or manor by the castle.

Castor (Ca): Roman fort.

Caswell (Do, Nth, O): Cress spring.

Catcleugh (Nb): Wild-cat ravine.

Caterham (Sr): ?Homestead by the fort; ?Homestead by the chair-shaped hill.

Catford (Lo): (Wild) cat ford.

Catforth (La): (Wild) cat ford.

Catley (H & W, L, GM): (Wild) cat wood.

Catterick (YN): ?Waterfalls; ?Hill fort; ?(Place of) battle ramparts.

Caughall (Ch): Hill of the cocks or fowl.

Causeway (O, W): Raised way.

Cavendish (Sf): Cafna's enclosure.

Cawkeld (Hm): Cold spring.

Cawkhill (YW): Cold spring.

Cawood (La, YN): Jackdaw wood.

Cawton (YN): Calf farm.

Cerne (river) (Do): Rocky stream.

Cerne Abbas (Do): Rocky stream place with an abbey.

Chaddesden (Db): Chad's valley.

Chadstone (Nth): Chad's farm or enclosure.

Chadwell (Lo): Cold spring.

Chadwick (Mr, WM): Chad's village.

Chagford (D): Broom ford.

Chaldon (Do): Calf hill.

Chalfont (Bk): ?Ceadel's spring; ?Calf spring.

Chalford (Gl, W): Chalk or limestone ford.

Chalk Farm (Lo): Same as **Caldecote**.

Chalton (Bd): Calf farm.

Chapel-en-le-Frith (Db): Chapel in the forest.

Chapmanslade (W): Merchants' valley.

Char (river) (Do): Rocky river.

Chard (So): Rough ground.

Charing Cross (K, Lo): Cross at a (river) bend.

Charlbury (O): Fort of Ceorl's people.

Charlcot(e): (common): Cottage(s) of the churls or free peasants.

Charl(e)ton (common): Farm or enclosure of the free peasants.

Charn (river) (Brk): Rocky river.

Charnwood (Le): ?Wood with a cairn; ?Rocks wood.

Charterhouse (Lo): Monastery of the Carthusians.

Chartwell (K): Spring in a rough common.

Chastleton (O): Farm or enclosure by the cashel or old stone fort.

Chatham (Ess, K): Forest homestead.

Chatsworth (Db): Ceatt's farm or enclosure.

Chatteris (Ca): ?Forest stream.

Chawton (Ha): Calf farm.

Cheadle (GM, St): Forest or wood.

Cheam (Lo): Homestead by the tree stumps.

Cheap Street (common): Market street or place.

Cheddar (So): ?Ravine; ?Caverns.

Chedworth (Gl): Cedda's enclosure.

Cheetham (GM): Homestead in the wood.

Chelmer (river) (Ess): Back-formation from **Chelmsford**.

Chelmsford (Ess): Ceolmaer's ford.

Chelsea (Lo): Landing-place for chalk or limestone.

Cheltenham (Gl): ?Homestead by the hill.

Cheriton (common): Farm by or belonging to a church.

Chertsey (Sr): Cerot's island.

Cherwell (O): Winding river.

Chesham (Bk, GM): Homestead by a fort.

Cheshire: Shire ruled from Chester (q.v.).

Cheshunt (Hrt): Spring by a Roman fort.

Chesil Bank (Do): Shingle or gravel bank.

Chessington (Lo): Cissa's hill.

Chester (Ch, Db): Roman fort or city.

Chesterfield (Db, St): Open country of the Roman fort.

Chester-le-Street (Du): Roman fort by the Roman Road.

Chesterton (common): Farm by a Roman fort.

Cheviot (Nb): Meaning is unexplained.

Chew (GM, YW): Narrow valley.

Chichester (WS): Cissi's Roman fort.

Chickward (H & W): Chicken enclosure.

Chideock (Do): Wooded place.

Chiddingstone (K): ?Stone of Cidd's people.

Chilham (K): Homestead of Cilla's people.

Chillingham (Nb): Homestead of Ceofel's people.

Chilmark (W): Pole marking a boundary.

Chiltern (Brk): Hills.

Chilton (common): Farm of the junior noblemen or younger sons.

Chine (common): Ravine.

Chingford (Lo): Shingly ford.

Chinnor (O): ?Ceonna's hillside.

Chipley (So): Wood from which logs are cut.

Chippenham (Gl, Sf, W): Cippa's enclosure or water meadow.

Chipping (common): Market, market town.

Chipping Barnet (Lo): Market of Barnet.

Chipping Camden (Gl): Market of Camden.

Chipping Norton (O): Market of Norton.

Chipping Ongar (Ess): Market of Ongar.

Chipping Sudbury (Gl): Market of Sudbury.

Chipstead (W): Market place.

Chislehurst (Lo): Gravel hill.

Chiswick (Ca, Lo): Cheese farm.

Chittlehampton (D): Farm of the valley dwellers.

Chopwell (T & W): Well at which a market is held.

Chor (river) (La): ?Rocky river.

Chorley (Ch, La, Sa, St): Wood or clearing of the free peasants (churls).

Chorlton (Ch, GM, St): Farm or enclosure of the free peasants (churls).

Chudleigh (D): Ciedda's wood or clearing.

Chulmleigh (D): Ceolmund's wood or clearing.

Churchill (common): Occasionally 'little church'; mostly 'church hill'; also simply 'hill' (a Celtic element meaning 'hill' to which Old English 'hyll' is added).

Churston (D): Village with a church.

Cinderford (Gl): Cinder ford.

Cirencester (Gl): Roman fort of Corinium (place of the Cornovii).

Clacton (Ess): Farm or enclosure of Clacc's people.

Clapham (Bd, Lo, YN): Homestead on a hill or hillock.

Clapton (common): Farm on a hill or hillock.

Clare (Sf): ?Flat land.

Clavering (Ess): Clover field.

Claverton (Ch): Clover farm or enclosure.

Claydon (Bd, O, Sf): Clay hill.

Clayhanger (D, So, WM): Clayey slope.

Clayton (common): Clay farm or enclosure (on clay soil).

Cleator (Cu): Rocky (?) shieling.

Cleckheaton (YW): Farm or enclosure on a hill or high ground.

Clee (common): Cliffs.

Cleethorpes (Hm): ?Outlying village or farm with clayey soil.

Cleeve (common): Hill or slope, steep slope, cliff.

Clehonger (H & W): Clayey slope.

Cleobury (Sa): Fort by the Clee hills.

Clerkenwell (Lo): Spring of the clerics.

Clevedon (So): Hill with cliffs.

Cleveland: Hilly district.

Cliff(e) (common): Slope, steep slope, escarpment, cliff.

Clifford (common): Ford at a slope.

Clinger (Do): Clayey slope.

Clint(s) (common): Hill.

Clitheroe (La): Hill of loose stones.

Clive (common): Same as cliff.

Cliveden (Bk): Valley among cliffs.

Clopton (common): Farm on a hill or hillock.

Clotton (Ch): Farm or enclosure in a ravine.

Clough (common): Ravine, valley.

Cloughton (YN): Farm or enclosure in a ravine.

Clovelly (D): Ravine on the round ridge.

Clowne (Db): Hill by the (river) Clun.

Clumber (Nth): Hill above the river.

Clun (Sa): See **Colne**.

Coalville (Le): Coal town.

Coat(e)(s) (common): Hut(s), cottage(s), shed(s), shelter(s).

Co(a)tham (common): (Place of) cottages or shelters.

Cobham (Sr): Cofa's homestead.

Cocker (river) (Cu, YN): Crooked river.

Cockerington (L): Farm of the Cocker (river) dwellers.

Cockersand (La): Sandy bank of the Cocker.

Cockey (La): Enclosure of the wild birds.

Cockfosters (Lo): Place of the head forester.

Cockshot, Cockshutt(s) (common): Place of cock-shooting (i.e., where nets are spread to catch woodcock).

Codsall (St): Cod's nook of land.

Coggeshall (Ess): Cogg's corner of land.

Colburn (YN): Cold spring.

Colchester (Ess): ?Roman fort on the (river) Colne; ?Roman city of Colonia (town of Roman citizens).

Coldcoats (La, Nb, YN): Cold huts.

Coldharbour (common): Shelter from cold or bitter weather (one without a fire).

Cold Keld (YN): Cold spring.

Coleshill (Bk, O): Hill.

Colindale (La): Colin's valley.

Colman Hargos (YN): Colman's shelter or summer pasture.

Coln (river) (Gl): Meaning is unexplained, possibly 'water'.

Colne (Ess): See **Coln**.

Colne (La): Place on the (river) Colne.

Colne (river) (La): ?Roaring river, water.

Colney (H & W, Nf): Cola's island.

Colsterdale (YN): Valley of the charcoal-burners.

Colsterworth (L): Farm of the charcoal-burners.

Coltishall (Nf): Cohede's or Coccede's corner of land.

Colwall (Hrt): Cold spring.

Colwell (Nb, IW): Cold spring.

Colworth (Bd, WS): Cula's farm or enclosure.

Colyton (D): Farm or enclosure on the Coly ('narrow river').

Comb, Combe, Coombe (common): Narrow valley.

Combridge (St): Ridge crest.

Combs (Cu, Db, Sf): Hill crests.

Compton (common): Farmstead in a narrow valley.

Condover (Sa): ?Hound river-place.

Coney Geer (Nth): Rabbit warren.

Coneygrey (Nt): Rabbit warren.

Congleton (Ch): ?Farm or enclosure by the round hill.

Conigree (Hrt): Rabbit warren.

Coningsby (L): King's village.

Conisbrough (YS): King's fort.

Coniston (Cu, Hm, YN): King's manor.

Conkesbury (Db): Crane fort.

Consett (Du): High hill.

Cookham (Brk): Hill farm.

Copeland (Cu): Bought land.

Copford (Ess): Coppa's ford.

Copmanthorpe (YN): Merchant's (chapman's) farm.

Copp (La): Hill, hill-top.

Coppull (La): Peaked hill.

Coquet (Nb): Cock wood.

Corbridge (Nb): Bridge at Corstopitum (Roman fort and supply station for Hadrian's Wall).

Corby (Cu): Corc's village.

Corby (L, Nth): Kori's village.

Coreley (Sa): Slope where cranes are found.

Corfe (Do, So): Gap, pass.

Corhampton (Ha): Corn farm on a river meadow.

Corley (Wa): Wood or clearing of the cranes.

Cornbrook (La): Crane brook.

Cornforth (Du): Ford frequented by cranes.

Cornwall: The promontory people who are Welsh or Celtic.

Cornwood (D, H & W): Crane wood.

Corringham (Ess): Homestead of Curra's people.

Corse (Gl, H & W, So): Marsh, bog.

Corsham (W): Cosa's homestead.

Corsley (W): Marsh clearing.

Coseley (St): The charcoal-burner's wood.

Cosford (Sf): ?Marshy ford; ?Cosa's ford.

Cosford (Wa): Cosa's ford.

Cote (common): See **Coate(s)**.

Cotswolds (Gl): Cod's forest or upland.

Cottam (Db, La, Nt, Hm): (Place at) the cottages.

Cottenham (Ca): Cotta's homestead.

Cottesmore (Le): Cott's moor.

Cottingham (Nth, Hm): Homestead of Cotta's people.

Cottingley (YW): Forest or clearing of Cotta's people.

Cot(t)on (common): (Place of) cottages, cottage farm.

Coulsdon (Lo): Cuthred's hill.

Coulston (W): Cufel's farm or enclosure.

Countisbury (D): Hill fort.

Cove (D, Ha, Sf): Cove, sea inlet.

Covenham (L): ?Cofa's village; Village in a recess.

Coventry (WM): Cofa's tree.

Cowden (L, Hm): Woodland pasture for cows.

Cowes (IW): ?Cows.

Cowfield (common): Open country with cows.

Cowfold (K, St, WS): Cow fold, enclosure.

Cowhill (Db): Cow hill.

Cowleaze (common): Cow pasture.

Cowley (Gl): Cow pasture.

Cowley (Bk, D, Lo, O): Cofa's wood or clearing.

Cowling (La, YN): Pasture by the hill.

Coxwold (YN): Cuha's high forest land.

Crackpot (YN): Crow or raven pit.

Cracoe (YN): Spur of land frequented by crows.

Cramlington (Nb): Crane-spring farm.

Cranbo(u)rne (Brk, Do): Crane stream.

Cranbrook (K): Crane brook.

Cranfield (Bd): Open country with cranes.

Cranford (Lo, Nth): Ford of the cranes or herons.

Cranham (Lo): Ridge where crows are plentiful.

Crankshaw (La): ?Corn copse; ?Crane copse.

Cranleigh (Sr): Crane wood.

Cranmore (IW, So): Crane pool.

Craven (YN): Place of wild garlic.

Crawley (common): Crow wood.

Crediton (D): Farm or manor on (the river) Creedy.

Creech (Do): Hill, rock.

Creswell (Db, Nb, St): Cress spring.

Crewe (Ch): Ford, stepping stones.

Crewkerne (So): House at the hill.

Crich (Db): Hill.

Crichel (Do): Hill.

Cricket (So): Hill, rock.

Cricklade (W): Hill passage.

Crickle (YW): Hill.

Cricklestone (YW): Stone hill.

Cricklewood (Lo): Hill, rounded hill.

Cringledike (Cu): Ring ditch.

Cringleford (Nf): Round or curved ford.

Crisbrook (K): Brook abounding in cress.

Croft (common): Piece of enclosed land (with a building).

Crofton (common): Farm with a small, enclosed field.

Cromer (Hrt, Nf): Crow lake.

Cromford (Db): Ford at a bend.

Crompton (La): Farm at the river bend.

Cromwell (Nt, YW): Winding stream.

Crondall (Ha): Quarry, chalk-pit.

Crook(s) (common): A bend (usually land at a river bend); (Occasionally) a hill.

Crook Hill (Db): 'Crook' means 'hill'.

Croome (H & W, So): Land along a winding stream.

Crosby (common): Village with (rood) crosses.

Crossthwaite (Cu, YN): Stone cross in a clearing.

Crowborough (St, ES): Crow hill.

Crowcombe (So): Crow valley.

Crowhurst (Sr, ES): ?Wooded hill of the crows; ?Saffron hill.

Crowland (L, Sf): Land at a (river) bend.

Crowle (H & W, Hm): Winding stream.

Crowndale (D): Quarry or chalk-pit valley.

Crowthorne (Brk): ?Thorny place of the crows; ?Thorn tree of the crows.

Croxteth (La): Krokr's landing place.

Croxton (common): Krokr's farm or enclosure.

Croydon (Ca): Crow valley.

Croydon (So): Crow hill.

Croydon (Lo): Saffron valley.

Crummock Water (Cu): Winding water.

Crumpsall (GM): Crum's water meadow.

Crundale (K): ?Valley; ?Chalk-pit.

Crundall (H & W): ?Valley with a quarry or chalk-pit.

Cuckfield (WS): ?Open country with cuckoos; ?Open country with couch grass.

Cuddesdon (O): Cuthen's hill.

Cudham (Lo): Cuda's homestead.

Cudworth (YS): Cutha's enclosure.

Cuffley (Hrt): Cofa's (?) wood or clearing.

Culcheth (Ch): Back-wood, wood at the back.

Cullercoats (T & W): Dove cotes.

Cullompton (D): Farm or enclosure on the (river) Cullum (?'winding river').

Culverden (K): Woodland pasture frequented by doves.

Culverhouse (common): Dove house.

Culverton (Bk): Dove hill.

Cumberland: Land of the Welsh.

Cumnor (O): Cuma's or Colman's hill slope.

Cut(t)mill (common): Mill with cut or man-made stream.

Cuttle (So, Wa): Water channel.

Dacorum (Hrt): (District) belonging to the Danes.

Dacre (YN): Water.

Dacre Beck (Cu): Water/stream. (A Norse element meaning 'stream' was added to the old Celtic word of the same meaning.)

Dagenham (Lo): Daecca's homestead.

Dalby (L, Le, YN): Village in a hill valley.

Dalston (Lo): Deorlaf's farm or enclosure.

Dalston (Cu): ?Dall's farm; ?Farm in a valley.

Dalton (common): Farm or enclosure in a valley.

Danby (YN): Village of the Danes.

Darent (river) (K): Oak river.

Darenth (K): Named from the river.

Darfield (YS): Open country with deer.

Darlaston (St, WM): Deorlaf's farm or enclosure.

Darley (common): Deer wood.

Darlington (Du): The farm or enclosure of Deornoth's people.

Dart (river): Oak river.

Dartford (K): Ford over the (river) Darent.

Dartington (D): Farm or enclosure of the dwellers by the (river) Dart.

Dartmoor (D): Moor of (the river) Dart.

Dartmouth (D): Mouth of (the river) Dart.

Darwen (La): Oak river.

Daventry (Nth): Dafa's tree.

Dawlish (D): Black stream.

Deadwin Clough (La): Ravine of the dead woman (where a corpse was found?).

Deal (K): Valley.

Dean(e) (common): Valley, especially wooded valley.

Deddington (O): Farm or enclosure of Daeda's people.

Dedham (Ess): Dydda's homestead.

Dee (river) (Cu, YN): ?Goddess, holy river.

De(e)pdale (common): Deep valley.

Deeping (Ca, L): Deep fen.

Deerfold (H & W): Deer fold or enclosure.

Deerhurst (Gl): Wooded hill where deer are found.

Delf, Delph (common): Quarry.

Dembleby (L): Valley with a stream.

Den (common): A swine pasture.

Denby (Db): Village of the Danes.

Dene (common): Same as 'Dean'.

Denge (K): Valley district.

Denge Marsh (K): Marsh in the valley district.

Denham (Bd, Sf): Homestead in a valley.

Denholme (YW): Water meadow in a valley.

Dent (Cu, YW): ?(Place by) a hill.

Denton (common): Farm or enclosure in a valley.

Denver (Nf): Passage of the Danes.

Deptford (Lo, T & W): Deep ford.

Derby: Village where deer are found.

Dereham (Nf): Homestead where deer are found.

Derwent (river) (Cu, Db, Hm, Nb): Oak river.

Desborough (Nth): Deor's fort.

Dethick (Db): Death oak (tree on which felons were hanged).

Devenham (Sf): ?Homestead on the deep river.

Devizes (W): Boundary (between two 'hundreds').

Devon: A name from Defnas/Dumnonii, which was transferred from earlier Celtic colonists to their Saxon conquerors (it may mean 'the deep ones', a reference to mining).

Devonport (D): Devon harbour.

Dewsbury (YW): Dewi's (David's) fort.

Didcot (O): Duda's cottage.

Didsbury (GM): Dyddi's fort.

Dimple(s) (GM, YW): Pool in a wood or valley.

Dingle (Gl, Mr, Wa): A dell or deep dell.

Dingley (Nth): Wood in a valley.

Dinglewell (Gl): Spring in a dell.

Dinnington (So, YS): Farm of Dinn's or Dunna's people.

Dinton (Bk, W): Dunna's farm or enclosure.

Dishforth (YN): Ford by a dyke or ditch or drainage channel.

Disley (GM): Forest or clearing by a dyke.

Diss (Nf): Ditch.

Ditchling (ES): (Place of) Diccel's people.

Ditton (common): Farm surrounded by a moat or by a ditch; farm near or with a ditch.

Dod(d)ington (common): Farm or enclosure of Dodda's or Dudda's people.

Dogbury (Do): Dog hill.

Don (river) (YS): ?Rapid river; ?Brown river; ?River.

Doncaster (YW): Roman fort on the (river) Don (i.e., the Roman fort called Dano).

Don(n)ington (common): ?Farm or enclosure of Dunn's people; ?Place by a hill.

Dorchester (Do, O); Roman city (in the place) of the Durotriges (?'people of the pebbly place').

Dore (Hrt, YS): Water place.

Dorfold (Ch): Deer enclosure or fold.

Dorking (Sr): ?Dwellers on (the river) Dork; ?Place of Deorc's people.

Dorney (Bk): Humble-bee island.

Dorrington (Sa): Farm of Dodda's people.

Dorset: Settlers around Dorn.

Doughton (Gl, Nf): Duck farm or enclosure.

Douglas (river) (GM, La): Black stream.

Dove (river) (Db, YN, YW): Black river.

Dovedale (Db): Valley of the (river) Dove ('black river').

Dovehouse (common): Dove house.

Dover (K): (Place at) the waters.

Dovercourt (Ess): Water or river, plus 'corte' (last element is unexplained).

Down(e) (common): Hill or slope.

Downham (common): Hill homestead.

Downham (La, Nb): (Place) by the hills.

Downside (So, Sr): Hill side.

Downton (common): Hill farm.

Drakedale (YN): Dragon's valley.

Drakehill (Sr): Dragon hill.

Drakelow (Bd, Db, H & W): Dragon mound.

Draycot(t), Draycote (common): Cottages by a place of portage, often a tongue of land between streams or waterways.

Drayton (common): Farm by a place of portage.

Drewsteignton (D): Farm on the (river) Teign held by Drogo.

Driffield (Gl, Hm): Open country with stubble.

Dringhouses (YN): Houses of the free tenants.

Drinsey (L, Nt): Grazing enclosure of the free tenants.

Droitwich (H & W): Dirty place with buildings for storing salt.

Dronfield

Dronfield (Db): Open country with drones.

Droylesden (GM): Valley of the dry stream.

Duckworth (La): Duck enclosure.

Duddington (Nth): Farm of Dudda's people.

Dudley (common): Dudda's wood or clearing.

Duffield (Db, YN): Open country frequented by doves.

Dufton (Cu): Dove farm.

Dukinfield (GM): Open country frequented by ducks.

Dullingham (Ca): Homestead of Dulla's people.

Dulverton (So): ?Farm by the ford.

Dulwich (Lo): Marshy meadow where dill or vetch grows.

Dumplington (GM): Farm by a pool in a wood or valley.

Dungeness (K): Marsh of the valley district.

Dunmail Raise (Cu): Cairn of Dunmail (a tenth-century prince of Strathclyde).

Dunmow (Ess): Hill meadow.

Dunnose (IW): Nose hill (hill shaped like a nose).

Dunsfold (Sr): Dunt's fold or enclosure.

Dunsford (Lo): Ford in a valley.

Dunstable (Bd): Dunna's post or pillar.

Dunster (So): Dunn's torr or rocky peak or hill.

Duntish (Do): ?Hill that has grazing places.

Dunton (common): Hill farm.

Dunwich (Sf): Deep harbour.

Durfold (Co, Sr): Deer fold or enclosure.

Durham: Island on a hill.

Durley (Ha, W): Deer wood.

Durrington (Sr, W): Farm of Deora's people.

Dursley (Gl): Deorsige's wood or clearing.

Durston (So): Deor's farm or enclosure.

Dwariden (YW): Valley of the dwarfs.

Dwerryhouse (La): House of the dwarfs.

Dymchurch (K): ?Diuma's church; ?Church of the judge.

Eaglescliffe (Cle): Hillside where eagles are found.

Ealing (Lo): (Place of) Gilla's people.

Eamont (Cu): Meeting or confluence of waters.

Eardisland (H & W): The earl's place in Leon (?rivers) district.

Eardisley (H & W): Aegheard's forest or clearing.

Earith (Ca): Gravelly landing-place.

Earlestown (Mr): The town was called after Sir Hardman Earle, a railway company director. It grew up around a railway wagon-works.

Earl's Barton (Nth): Barley farm belonging to the Earl (of Huntingdon).

Earl's Croome (H & W): Land at a river bend owned by the Earl (of Warwick).

Earlshaw (Nth): Earl's wood.

Easby (YN): Ese's village.

Easington (Bk, Du, YN, YW): Farm or enclosure of Esa's or Esi's people.

Eastbourne (Du, ES): Place east of the stream.

Eastcot(e) (common): Eastern cottages or huts.

Easingwold (YN): Woodland of Esa's people.

Easter (common): Sheep fold.

Eastham (common): Eastern homestead or river-meadow.

43

Eastington (D, Do, Du, Gl, H & W): Eastern part of the village.

Eastleach (Gl): East stream.

Eastleigh (D): East wood or clearing.

Eastnor (H & W): East of the ridge.

Eastoft (Hm): East house or buildings.

Easton (common): Eastern enclosure or village.

Eastover (So): Eastern riverbank.

Eastry (K): The easterly region (of Kent).

Eaton (common): Farm by a river (occasionally: farm on an island or water-meadow).

Eau (H & W, Nf): River, stream.

Ebchester (Du): Ebba's Roman fort.

Eccles (common): Church (place), often referring to a church of Celtic foundation.

Ecclesall (YW): ?Eccel's corner of land; ?Piece of land with a church.

Ecclesfield (YS): Open country on which stands a church.

Eccleshall (St): Corner of land on which stands a church.

Eccleshill (La, YW): Church hill.

Eccleston (La, Mr): Enclosure or village with a church.

Eckington (Db, H & W): Farm associated with or belonging to Ecca or Ecci.

Edale (Db): Land between streams.

Eden (Cu): ?Hillside; ?Gushing river.

Edenbridge (K): Eadhelm's or Eadwulf's bridge.

Edgbaston (WM): Ecgbald's enclosure or farm.

Edge (common): Sharp ridge or escarpment, edge, hillside.

Edgefield (Nf): Park enclosure in open country.

Edgeley (Ch, Sa): Enclosure in a wood clearing.

Edgeworth (La, Gl): Enclosure on a hillside.

Edgware (Lo): Ecgi's weir.

Edington (Nb): Enclosure or farm of Ida's people.

Edington (W): Uncultivated hill.

Edmonton (Lo): Eadhelm's enclosure or farm.

Eelmere (YS): Eel pool.

Effingham (Sr): Homestead of Effa's people.

Egham (Sr): Ecga's enclosure or homestead.

Egremont (Cu): Named from Aigremont in
    Normandy; Hill by the (river) Ehen.

Eldmire (YN): Swan lake.

Eldwick (YW): Helgi's dwelling or farm.

Elham (K): ?Eel village or homestead.

Elkstone (St): Ealac's hill.

Elland (YW): Island or land by water.

Ellerbeck (Cu, La, YN): Alder-tree stream.

Ellershaw (Cu): Alder-tree wood.

Ellerton (Sa): Athelheard's farm or enclosure.

Ellerton (Hm, YE, YN): Alder-tree farm.

Ellesmere (Sa): Elli's lake.

Elloughton (Hm): ?Shrine on a hill.

Elmet (YW): Meaning is unexplained.

Elmbridge (Sr): Bridge over the misty river.

Elmham (Nf, Sf): Elm homestead.

Elmley (H & W, K): Elm wood.

Elmstead (Lo, K): Place of elms.

Elsage (Bk): Elm hedge.

Elsdon (Nb): Ellis valley.

Elsenham (Ess): Elsa's homestead.

45

Elste(a)d (Sr, WS): Place of elders.

Elstob (Du): (Place of) elder-tree stumps.

Elstow (Bd): Aellen's place or dairy farm.

Elstree (Hrt): Tidwulf's tree.

Elterwater (La): Swan lake.

Eltham (Lo): Elta's homestead.

Elton (common): Ella's enclosure or farm.

Elvetham (Ha): Water meadow frequented by swans.

Ely (Ca): Eel district.

Embleton (Nth): Aemele's farm or enclosure.

Emmetts, Emmott (Brk, Db, K): Confluence of waters, junction of rivers or streams.

Empingham (Le): Homestead of Empa's people.

Emsworth (Ha): Aemele's enclosure.

Enborne (Brk): Stream frequented by ducks.

Endcliffe(e) (Db, YS): Sloping ground frequented by ducks.

Enfield (H & W, Lo): ?Open country with lambs; ?Eana's open country.

England: Land of the Anglians, Angles, English men.

Englebourne (D): Stream of the Angles.

Englefield (Brk): Open country of the Angles.

Ennerdale (Cu): Anund's valley.

Entwistle (La): River fork frequented by ducks.

Epping (Ess): (Place of) the dwellers of the upland.

Epsom (Sr): Ebbe's homestead.

Epworth (Hm): Eoppa's enclosure.

Erdington (WM): Enclosure of Eored's or Eanred's people.

Eridge (ES): Eagle ridge.

Erith (K): Gravelly landing place.

Escombe (Du): (Place of) parks or enclosures.

Escrick (YN): ?Narrow strip; ?Stream; ?Ditch with ash trees.

Esher (Sr): Meaning uncertain, possibly connected with ash trees.

Esholt (YW): Ash-tree wood.

Eshott (Nb): Ash-tree grove.

Esk (river) (Cu, YN): Water.

Eskdale (Cu): Valley of the (river) Esk.

Essex: (Place of the) East Saxons.

Eston (Cle): Eastern enclosure or farm.

Etchells (Ch, Db): Land added to an estate or village.

Eton (Bk): River farm.

Euston (Lo, Sf): Eof's farm or enclosure.

Everley (YN): Boar wood.

Everton (Bd, Ha, Mr, Nt): Boar farm.

Evesham (H & W): ?Eof's homestead; ?Eof's river-meadow.

Ewell (K, Sr): Source of a stream or spring.

Ewelme (O): Source of a stream or spring.

Ewen (Gl): ?Cress spring; ?Source of a stream or spring.

Ewhurst (Ha, Sr, ES): ?Wooded hill; ?Copse of yew trees.

Exe (river) (So, D): Water.

Exeter (D): Roman city on the (river) Exe.

Exmouth (D): Mouth of the Exe.

Exton (Ha): (Place of the) farm of the East Saxons.

Eyam (Db): (Place of) islands.

Eye (common): Island.

Eye Brook (Le): Land surrounded by water.
Eynsford (K): Aegen's ford.
Eynsham (O): ?Aegen's homestead; ?Aegen's water-meadow.

Failsworth (GM): ?Enclosure made of hurdles.
Fairford (Gl): Clear-water ford.
Fairley (Sa): Clearing with ferns.
Fairlight (ES): Clearing with ferns.
Fakenham (Nf, Sf): Facca's homestead.
Faldingworth (Le): Enclosure by or with a fold.
Falkland (common): Folk land, from which the king draws rents and customary services; see **Faulkland.**
Falmer (ES): ?Fallow land by the sea.
Falmouth (Co): Mouth of the (river) Fal (?'river with steep banks').
Fareham (Ha): Fern homstead.
Faringdon (Brk, Do, Ha, O): Fern hill.
Farleigh (**Farley**) (common): Clearing with ferns.
Farnborough (Brk, Ha, La, Wa): Fern hill.
Farndale (YN): Fern valley.
Farndish (Bd): Fern parkland.
Farndon (Ch, Nt): Fern hill.
Farne Islands (Nb): Fern islands.
Farnham (common): Fern farm or homestead; (Occasionally) ferny river-meadow.
Farnham (Nb): (Place) by thorn bushes.
Far(n)ley (St, YW): Fern clearing.
Farnworth (Ch, GM): Fern enclosure.
Far(r)ington (Av, Brk, Do, La): Fern hill.
Farsley (YW): Furze clearing.

Farthinghoe (Nth): Dwellers among the ferns.

Faulkland (So): Land held by customary right or law (folk or people's land); see also **Falkland**.

Faversham (K): ?Faefer's enclosure or homestead; ?Smith's homestead.

Fawcett (Cu): Many-coloured hillside.

Fawley (Brk, Bk, Ha, H & W): Light-coloured clearing.

Faxton (Nth): Farm with rough grass.

Fazakerley (Mr): Plot on the edge of a wood.

Featherston(e) (Nb, St, YW): Four stones (burial stones).

Feckenham (H & W): Fecca's enclosure or homestead.

Felixstowe (Sf): ?Place of church dedicated to St Felix; ?Felica's religious building.

Felsted (Ess): Site in open country.

Feltham (Lo, Sr): Homestead in open country.

Felton (common): Farm in open country.

Fenby (L): Fen village or homestead.

Fenchurch (Lo): Church in the fen.

Fenton (common): Marsh farm.

Fenwick (Nb, YW): Buildings in or near a fen or marsh.

Fernworthy (D): Fern enclosure.

Ferrensby (YN): Place of the Faeroe Islander.

Ferriby (Hm): Village at the ferry.

Ferring (Ess, WS): (Place of) Fera's people.

Fifield (Brk, O, W): Holding of five hides (a hide denoted the amount of land needed to support a free household); see also **Huish**.

Filey (YN): The five forests or forest clearings.

Finchale (Du): Secluded place frequented by finches.
Fincham (Nf): Village frequented by finches.
Finchingfield (Ess): Finca's open country.
Finchley (Lo): Finch wood.
Finedon (Nth): Valley of the meetings or assemblies.
Finsbury (Lo): Fin's manor.
Firbank (Cu): Wooded hill-slope.
Firbeck (YS): Stream in a wood.
Firsby (L): Village of the Frisians.
Fishbourne (IW, WS): Fish stream, stream abounding in fish.
Fishlake (YS): Fish stream, stream abounding in fish.
Fishwick (La): Building constructed for dealing in fish.
Fitts (YN, YW): Grassland on the bank of a river.
Fitz (Sa): Grassland on the bank of a river.
Flagg (Db): ?Place where peat is cut; ?Place of water plants or flags.
Flamborough (Hm): Flein's fort.
Flash (St): A pool.
Flat Home (So): ?Island of the fleet.
Flaxley (Gl, YW): Clearing where flax is grown.
Flaxton (YN): Flax farm.
Fleet (common): (Place by) a creek or stream.
Fleetwood (La): Named from Sir Peter Hesketh-Fleetwood who founded it on a part of his estate in 1836.
Flegg (Nf): (Place of) water plants or flags.
Fletton (Hm): Farm or enclosure on a river bank.
Flitwick (Bd): Dairy farm by a stream.
Flixborough (L): Flik's fortified place.
Fold (common): Enclosure for animals.

Follifoot (YN): (Place of) horse-fighting and horse-racing.

Folkestone (K): Folca's stone.

Folkland (common): Folk land (land held by customary right or law); see also **Falkland**.

Fontmell (Do): Stream by a bare hill.

Forcett (YN): ?(Place by) a waterfall; ?Fold by a ford.

Ford (common): Ford, river-crossing.

Fordham (Ca, Ess, Nf): Homestead or enclosure by a ford.

Fordingbridge (Ha): Bridge of the ford-dwellers.

Foreland (D, IW, K): Foreland, headland, promontory.

Formby (La): ?The old village; ?Forni's village.

Foscote, Foscot(t) (common): Fox cottage.

Fosse Way: Road flanked by ditches.

Forstall, Forestal (common): A paddock or way to front of farmhouse.

Foston (common): Fot's farm or enclosure.

Fother (common): Odd scrap of land in open field.

Fotheringay (Nth): ?Island of Froda's people; ?Grazing island.

Foulness (Ess): Headland of the birds.

Fowey (Co): ?Beech river.

Fowlmere (Ca): Bird marsh.

Foxcote, Foxcot(t) (common): Fox cottage.

Foxholes (common): Fox-holes or earths.

Framilode (Gl): Passage (over the river Severn) at (the river) Frome.

Framlingham (Nf, Sf): Homestead of Framela's people.

Frampton (Av, Gl, L): Farm or enclosure on the (river) Frome.

Freckleton (La): ?Farm by the dangerous pool.

Frensham (Sr): Fremi's homestead or enclosure.

Freshford (Av): Ford with fresh or clear water.

Freshwater (IW): Fresh water (river).

Fressingfield (Sf): Open country where furze is abundant.

Freston (Sf): Enclosure of the Frisians.

Friern Barnet (Lo): Barnet belonging to the friars or brothers (Knights of St John of Jerusalem).

Friesthorpe (L): Village of the Frisians.

Frieston (L): Farm or village of the Frisians.

Frimley (Sr): Fremi's wood or clearing.

Fringford (O): ?Ford of the travellers.

Frinton-on-Sea (Ess): ?Enclosed farm by the sea; ?Fritha's farm.

Friskney (L): ?Fresh-water island; ?Fresh-water river.

Friston (Sf, ES): Farm of the Frisians.

Frith, Thrift (common): A wood.

Frithsden (Hrt): Wooded valley.

Fritton (Nf, Sf): Enclosed farm or village.

Frodsham (Ch): Frod's enclosure or farm.

Frogmore (common): Frog pool.

Frome (Gl): ?Fair or brisk river.

Frostenden (Sf): Valley where frogs are numerous.

Frosterley (Du): Wood or clearing of the foresters.

Froxfield (Ha, W): Open country where frogs are numerous.

Fryston (YW): Village of the Frisians.

Fuggelstone (W): Fugol's farm or enclosure.
Fulford (common): Foul or muddy ford.
Fulham (Lo): Fulla's river-meadow.
Fullamoor (D): Moor of the foals.
Fulmer (Bk): Marsh of the birds.
Fulshaw (Ch): Bird wood.
Fulstone (YW): Fugol's farm or enclosure.
Furness (La): Headland opposite Futh (rump) Island, now called Piel Island (this last name means 'island with a fortified tower').
Furze (Co, D): Place where furze is abundant.
Fyfield (common): Holding of five hides (see **Fifield**).
Fylde (La): Plain.

Gaddesby (Le): Gaddr's village.
Gaddesden (Hrt): ?Valley of the kid goats; ?Gaete's valley.
Gadshill (K): God's hill.
Gainsborough (L): Gegn's fort.
Galligill (Cu): Gallows hill.
Gappah (D): Goat path.
Garforth (YW): ?Gaera's ford; ?Ford on a triangular piece of land.
Gargrave (YN): ?Grove on a triangular strip of land.
Garsdon (W): Grassy hill.
Garsington (O): (Place of plentiful) grass, grazing place.
Garstang (La): ?Spear pole (?boundary marker).
Garston (GM): Large stone.
Garth (common): Close, garden.
Gatcomb(e) (So, IW): Goat valley.

Gateley (Nf): Goat clearing.
Gatesbury (Hrt): Fort of the goats.
Gatesgill (Cu): Goat shelter.
Gateshead (T & W): Goat headland.
Gatwick (WS): ?Goat farm.
Gawber (YS): Gallows hill.
Gawsworth (Ch): Gof's (smith's) farm or enclosure.
Gawthorpe (YW): Gauk's farm.
Gedling (Nt): (Place of) Gedel's people.
Giggleswick (YN): Gikel's building.
Gillingham (Do, K, Nf): Homestead of Gylla's people.
Gilsland (Nb): Gillie's land.
Gisburn (La): ?Rushing or gushing stream.
Glastonbury (So): Fort of the Glaestingas (from Glastone, a Celtic name associated with woad according to some authorities, but the meaning is uncertain).
Gledhill (YW): Kite (the bird) hill.
Gledhow (YW): Kite (the bird) hill.
Glossop (Db): Glott's small valley.
Gloucester (Gl): Roman fort of Glevum (?'bright place').
Glusburn (YN): Glistening stream.
Glyndebourne (ES): Enclosure by a stream.
Glynleigh (ES): Enclosure in a clearing.
Gnatham (Co, D): Water-meadow of the gnats.
Godalming (Sr): (Place of) Godhelm's people.
Godley (GM, Sr): Goda's wood or clearing.
Godmanchester (Ca): Godmund's (Roman) fort.
Godney (So): Goda's island.

Godsfield (Ha): ?Field or open country of God.

Godshill (Ha, IW): ?Hill of God.

Godstow (O): Place of God (from a twelfth-century nunnery).

Godswell (Grove) (W): ?Spring of God.

Goldhard (common): Gold hoard or treasure (where such was found).

Good Easter (Ess): Godiva's sheep fold.

Goodrich (H & W): Godric's castle.

Goodwood (WS): Godgifu's (a woman's name) wood.

Goole (Hm): Ditch, stream.

Goosey (O): Goose island.

Gordale Scar (YN): Rocky cliff of the dirty valley.

Gore (W): Triangular plot or point of land.

Goring (O, WS): (Place of) Gara's people.

Gorleston (Nf): Gurl's (?) farm or enclosure.

Gorsley (Gl, Ch, H & W): Gorse clearing.

Gosford (D, H & W, WM): Goose ford.

Gosforth (Cu, T & W): Goose ford.

Gosport (Ha): Goose market.

Gotham (Nt): Goat homestead.

Goudhurst (K): Gutha's wooded hill.

Gowbarrow (Cu): ?Gallows mound; ?Windy hill.

Gowthorpe (Nf, La, Hm, YN): Gaukr's outlying or dependent farm.

Graf(f)ham (Ca, St, WS): Homestead by a grove.

Grafton (common): Grove farm or enclosure.

Grafty (K): Grass enclosure.

Grange-over-Sands (Cu): The grange above (Morecambe) sands.

Grantham

Grantham (L): ?Granta's enclosure or homestead; ?Gravelly homestead.

Grasmere (Cu): Grassy pool.

Grassendale (Mr): Grazing or grassy valley.

Grassington (YN): Grazing farm.

Grassthorpe (Nt): Outlying or dependent farm for grazing.

Gratton (D, Db, St): Great or large farm or enclosure.

Gravesend (K, Nth): End of the grove.

Gravesham (K): Homestead by the grove.

Grazeley (Brk): Wallowing-place for badgers.

Great Crosby (La): Large village with a cross.

Great Tey (Ess): Big enclosure or farm.

Great Wolford (Wa): ?Big rampart against wolves.

Greenhithe (K): Green landing-place.

Greenside (YN): Green hillside.

Greenwich (Lo): ?Green farm; ?Green trading-place.

Greetwell (L): Gravel spring.

Gresham (Nf): Grassy homestead.

Gressingham (La): Grazing farm.

Gretton (Sa): Farm on gravelly soil.

Greyfriars (O): Friary of the grey brothers or Franciscans.

Greystoke (Cu): Religious foundation on the (river) Cray.

Grimesthorpe (YS): Grimr's outlying farm.

Grimsby (L): Grimr's village.

Grim's Ditch or **Dyke** (Ha, YW and elsewhere): Grim's (another name for Woden) ditch.

Grimston (common): Grimr's farm or enclosure.

Grinstead (WS): Green place.
Grisedale (Cu): Valley of the young pigs.
Gristhwaite (YN): Clearing for young pigs.
Groombridge (K): Bridge of the boy or servant.
Groop (common): A sheep-pen.
Ground(s) (common): Stretch of land.
Grove (common): Grove.
Guildford (Sr): Ford of the golden flowers.
Guisborough (Cle): Gigr's (?) fort.
Guiseley (YW): Gislica's forest or clearing.
Guiting (Gl): Gushing spring.
Gumley (Le): Godmund's wood or clearing.
Gundisburgh (Sf): Stretch of land with a fort.
Gunnersbury (Lo): Gunnhild's (a woman's name) fort.
Gunnerside (YN): Gunnar's shieling.
Gutteridge (Lo): Great hedge.

Hackbridge (Lo): Bridge at a bend or hook-shaped piece of land.
Hackford (Nf): Ford at a river bend or hook-shaped piece of land.
Hackforth (YN): Ford at a river bend or hook-shaped piece of land.
Hackness (YN): Hook-nose headland.
Hackney (Lo): Haca's island or marsh.
Hackpen Hill (D, W): Hook-shaped hill.
Haddenham (Bk, Ca): Haeda's homestead.
Haddlesey (YW): Heathland (?) lake.
Haddon (Av, Db, Do, Nth): Heather hill.
Hadfield (Db): Open country with heather.

Hadleigh, Hadley

Hadleigh, Hadley (common): Heather clearing.

Hagg(s) (common): Place cleared of trees.

Hagley (H & W, Sa, So, St): ?Haw clearing; ?Haecga's wood or clearing.

Haigh (GM, YW): Grazing enclosure.

Hailey (Hrt, O): Hay or dried-grass clearing.

Haileybury (Hrt): Manor of Hailey.

Hailsham (ES): Haegel's homestead.

Hainault Forest (Lo): Wood of the religious community.

Hale(s) (common): Recess(es), remote corner(s) of land, nook(s).

Halesowen (WM): ?Owen's manor; ?Owen's corners of land.

Halesworth (Sf): Haele's enclosure or farm.

Halifax (YW): ?Slope with coarse grass; ?Nook with coarse grass.

Hallam (Db, YS): (Place) at or on rocky slopes.

Halling (Bk, K): (Place of) Healla's people.

Hallingbury (Ess): Fort of Heall's people.

Hallington (L): Healla's settlement.

Halliwell (GM): Holy well.

Halstead (Ess, K, Le): Temporary place of shelter (for cattle).

Halstead (La, L, YW): Place of a hall.

Haltemprice (YE): High enterprise.

Halton (common): Farm or enclosure in a secluded place.

Haltwhistle (Nb): High confluence of streams.

Halwell (Co, D): Holy well.

Halwill (D): Holy well.

Ham (common): Homestead (see Foreword, p. v).

Ham(m) (common): River-meadow, dry land in a marsh or by water, cultivated plot in marginal land (see Foreword, p. v).

Hamble (Ha): Crooked (river).

Hambledon (Do, Ha, Sr): Crooked or bare or cut-off hill.

Hambleton (YN): Hamela's farm or enclosure.

Hammersmith (Lo): Smithy of the hammer-maker.

Hampnett (Gl, WS): High farm.

Hampole (YS): Cock pool.

Hampreston (Do): Originally 'Ham', to which was added 'Preston'.

Hampshire: Named from Hammtun (former name of Southampton which meant low-lying land by a river).

Hampstead (common): Site of a dwelling, dwelling-place, manor.

Hampton (common): Three main meanings: 1, Farm by a homestead (home farm); 2, High farm; 3, Farm in a valley.

Hamsterley (Do): Corn-weevil clearing.

Han(d)ley (common): High wood or clearing.

Handsworth (YS, WM): ?Hun's or Handwulf's enclosure or farm.

Hanford (Ch, Do, St): Cock ford (i.e., moorhen).

Hanger Hill (Lo): Wood on a steep bank.

Hanwell (Lo, O): ?Hana's spring; ?Cock's spring.

Hanworth (Brk, Lo): ?Cock enclosure; ?Hana's enclosure.

Hanworth (Nf): Hagena's enclosure.

Harborough (Le): Hill of the oats.

Harborough (Wa): Earthwork fort.

Harbottle (Nb): Hired man's dwelling.

Harden (YW): Hare valley.

Hardwell (Brk): Treasure spring (where objects were cast).

Hardwick(e) (common): Farm with a herd or flock (sheep farm).

Haredene (W): Hare valley.

Harewood (common): Two meanings: 1, Grey wood; 2, Hare wood.

Harford (D): Army ford.

Haringey (Lo): Haering's enclosure in a wood.

Harland (YN): Barrow or cairn or shrine land.

Harlesden (Lo): Herewulf's farm or enclosure.

Harleston (D, Nf, Sf): Herewulf's farm or enclosure.

Harley (Sa, YS): ?Hare clearing; ?Grey, lichenous clearing.

Harlow (Ess, Nb): ?Scarped hill; ?Army hill or mound.

Harmondsworth (Lo): Heremod's enclosure.

Harome (YN): Barrows or cairns, shrines.

Harpenden (He): The harper's valley.

Harperwell (YW): ?The harper's spring; ?Nightingales' spring.

Harras (Cu): Cairn.

Harringay (Lo): ?Enclosure in the grey wood.

Harrington (Cu): Farm or enclosure of Haefer's people.

Harrogate (YN): ?The road to the grey hill; ?Pasture place of the grey hill; ?Pasture place by a barrow or cairn.

Harrow (Lo): Pagan shrine or temple.

Harrowden (Bd, Ess, Nth): Shrine on a hill.

Hartburn (Cle): Hart spring.

Harter Fell (Cu): Hill of the stags.

Hartford (Ca, Ch, Gl, Nb, So): Hart or stag ford.

Harthay (Ca): Part of wood fenced off for hunting deer.

Harthill (Ch, Db, YE, YS): Stag hill.

Hartland (D): Originally 'stag island'; 'land' was added later.

Hartlepool (Cle): The pool by Hart ('hart or stag island').

Hartley (Brk, Ha, K, So): Stag wood or clearing.

Hartlip (K): Leap-gate for stags (compare **Hindlip**).

Hartshead (GM, YW): Hart hill.

Hartshorne (Db): Stag headland.

Hartside (Cu, Nb): Hillside of the stags.

Hartwith (YN): Stag wood.

Harwell (Nt, O): Spring coming from the grey hill.

Harwich (Ess): Army camp.

Harwood (La): ?Grey wood; ?Hare wood.

Harworth (Nt): ?Stony enclosure.

Haseley (O, Wa, IW): Hazel wood.

Haslemere (Bk, Sr): Hazel pool.

Haslingden (La): Hazel valley.

Hastings (ES): (Place of) Haesta's people.

Hatch (Bd, Ha, So, W): Gate – usually to a park or forest.

Hatcham (Lo): Haecci's homestead.

Hatfield (common): Open country abounding in heather.

Hatherleigh

Hatherleigh (D): Hawthorn wood or clearing.

Hatherley (Gl): Hawthorn wood or clearing.

Hatherton (Ch, St): Hawthorn hill.

Hathersage (Db): ?Buck goat escarpment; ?Haefer's edge or escarpment.

Hatley (C, Bd): Wood on or by a hart-shaped hill.

Hatt (Co, Ha, W): Hat-shaped hill.

Hattersley (GM): Deer wood or clearing.

Hatton (common): Heath farm or enclosure.

Haugh (L, YS): Grazing enclosure.

Haughton (common): Enclosure in a secluded place or by low-lying land.

Hauxwell (YN): ?Hawk spring; ?Hafoc's spring.

Havant (Ha): Hama's spring.

Haverhill (Sf): Oat hill.

Haverigg (Cu): Oat ridge.

Havering (Lo): (Place of) Haefer's people.

Haw (Gl, O): Hedge, enclosure, property.

Hawes (YN): Neck of land, pass through hills.

Hawkhill (Nb): Hawk hill.

Hawkhurst (K): Hawk (wooded) hill.

Haw(k)ridge (Bk, Brk, So): Hawk ridge.

Hawkshead (Cu, La): Haukr's shieling or mountain pasture.

Hawksworth (Nt, YW): ?Hawk enclosure; ?Hauk's enclosure.

Haworth (YW): ?Haw enclosure; ?Hedge enclosure.

Haxey (Hm): Hakr's island.

Hay (common): Fence or enclosure, especially in woodland.

Haydock (Mr): Barley farm.

Haydon (Do, Nb, So, W): Hay hill or valley.

Hayes (D, Do): Fences.

Hayes (Gl, K, Lo): (Place of) brushwood.

Hayford (Nth, O): Hay ford.

Hayle (Co): Salt water.

Hayling (Ha): (Place of) Haegel's people.

Haymarket (Lo): Market specialising in hay.

Hayne(s) (D, Bd, K, L): Fence or area enclosed by a fence.

Hayton (Cu, Hrt, Nt, Sa): ?Farm surrounded by a hedge; ?Hay farm.

Haytor (D): Ivy (rocky) hill.

Haywards Heath (WS): Hedge enclosure on heather-covered land.

Haywood (H & W, Nt, Sa, St, YS): Enclosed wood.

Hazelslack (Cu): Hazel (shallow) valley.

Headingley (YW): Wood of Hede's people.

Headington (O): Hedena's hill.

Headley (common): Heather clearing.

Heanor (Db): (Place) by the high ridge.

Heap (GM): Hill.

Heath (common): A heath, heathery place.

Heathfield (common): Open, heather-covered country.

Heathrow (Lo): Row (of houses) on a heath.

Heaton (common): Farm on high land.

Heavitree (D): Head tree (probably meaning 'gallows').

Hebburn (T & W): High burial mound.

Hebden (YN, YW): Valley of the rose-hips.

Heckmondwike (YW): Heahmund's building or farm.

Hedon (Hm): Hill abounding in heather.

Helmdon (Nth): Helma's valley.

Helmsley (YN): Helm's wood or clearing.

Helstone (Co): Old court village.

Hemel Hempstead (Hrt): Homestead in broken country.

Hemsworth (YW): Hymel's enclosure.

Hendon (Du): Hind (female deer) valley.

Hendon (Lo, T & W): High hill.

Hendred (O): ?High thorn-tree wood; ?Waterfowl stream.

Henfield (WS): ?Open country with rocks; ?High, open country.

Henley (common): High wood or clearing.

Henshaw (YW): Copse of the wild birds.

Hensingham (Cu): ?(Place of) Hynsige's people.

Henstridge (So): Stallion ridge.

Henthorn (La): ?High thorn-tree wood; ?Thorn-tree wood where wild birds abound.

Heptonstall (YW): Stable or stall in Hebden.

Hereford: Army ford.

Herne (Ha, K, Lo): Angle, corner of land.

Herstmonceux (ES): Wooded hill of the Monceux family.

Hertford (Hrt, YN): Hart ford.

Hartsmere (Hrt): ?Hart pool.

Hesket (Cu): Ash-tree head or hill.

Hesket(h) (Cu, La, YN): Horse race-course.

Hesleden (Du, YN): Hazel valley.

Hestercombe (So): Valley of the minor nobleman.

Heston (Lo): Brushwood farm or enclosure.

Heswall (Mr): Hazel spring.
Hetton (Du, T & W, YN): Rose-hip hill.
Hever (K): High edge.
Hexham (Nb): Farm of the minor nobleman.
Hey (common): Fence, enclosure.
Heynings (L): Enclosed land.
Heysham (La): Brushland farm or enclosure.
Heytesbury (W): Heahthryth's fort.
Heywood (GM, W): ?Enclosed wood; ?High wood.
Hide (common): Measure of land sufficient to maintain a free family (see **Huish**).
Higham (common): High homestead.
Highbridge (Ha, So): High bridge.
Highbury (Lo, WS, YW): High fort or manor.
High Easter (Ess): High sheepfold.
Highfield(s) (common): Three meanings: 1, High, open country; 2, High, open spaces (in a wood); 3, High, enclosed space ('field' in modern sense).
High Force (Du, NY): High waterfall.
Highgate (Lo): High gate (a toll gate).
Highworth (W): High enclosure.
Hillingdon (Lo): Hilda's hill.
Hilton (common): Farm or enclosure on a hill.
Hinckley (Le): Hynca's wood or clearing.
Hindburn (La): Hind (female deer) stream.
Hinderclay (Sf): ?(Place of the) split tree-trunk; ?Hildr's wood or clearing.
Hindhead (Sr): Hind (female deer) hill.
Hindley (GM, Nb): Hind (female deer) wood.
Hindlip (H & W): Hind leap (leap-gate for hinds).

Hindon (W): Hill pasture of the religious community.

Hingham (Nf): High homestead.

Hinksey (O): ?Water meadow; ?Island of the stallions.

Hinton (common): In some cases 'high farm', in other cases 'farm of a religious community'.

Hirst (Nf, YW): Copse, wooded hill.

Hitchin (Hrt): (Place of) the Hicce people.

Hoath (K): Heathery place.

Hoathley (K, ES, WS): Heather clearing.

Hockley (Ch, Ess, St, Wm): ?Hocca's wood or clearing; ?Clearing of the mallows.

Hoddesdon (Hrt): Hod's hill.

Hodnet (Sa): Quiet valley.

Hoe (common): Spur of land.

Holbeach (common): Stream in a hollow.

Holbeck (Nt, YS, YW): Stream in a hollow.

Holborn (Lo): Stream in a hollow.

Holbrook (Db, Sf, YS): Stream in a hollow.

Holcombe (common): Deep, narrow valley.

Holderness (Hm): High-ranking yeoman's promontory.

Holkham (Nf): ?Homestead in a hollow.

Holland (Ess, La, L): Land by a hill spur.

Holloway (common): Two main meanings: 1, Track worn down to make a hollow; 2, Road or track in a hollow.

Hollywood (common): Holly wood.

Holme (common): Small island, river-meadow.

Holmfirth (YW): Wood belonging to Holme (a place whose name here means 'holly').

Holne (D): Place of holly.

Holsworthy (D): Heald's enclosure.

Holt (common): Wood, thicket.

Holwood (Lo): Wood in a hollow.

Homerton (Lo): Hunburg's (a woman's name) enclosure or farm.

Honeybourne (Gl, H & W): Honey stream (?sweet stream; ?yellow stream).

Honeychild (K): Huna's cold spring.

Honiton (D): Honey farm.

Hoo (K, Sf): Spur of land.

Hood (D, YN): ?Hood-shaped hill.

Hook(e) (common): Bend in a river or a hill; Hook-shaped place.

Hoole (Ch, La): Shed, hovel.

Hooley (Lo): Wood or clearing in a hollow.

Hope (common): Small, enclosed valley.

Hopton (common): Valley farm.

Hopwood (GM, H & W): Small, enclosed, wooded valley.

Horbury (YW): ?Dirty fort; ?Fort in a muddy place.

Hordle (Ha, Sa): Mount of the treasure.

Hordley (Sa): Wood of the treasure.

Horley (O, WS): Wood in a tongue of land.

Hornby (La, YN): Horni's village.

Horncastle (L): Roman fort on a tongue of land or river fork.

Hornchurch (Lo): Church with horns (gables).

Hornsby (Cu): Ormr's village.

Hornsea (Hm): Lake with horns or jutting pieces of land.

Hornsey (Lo): ?Grey wood enclosure.

Horsefield (common): Open country with horses.

Horsenden (Lo): ?Horsa's hill.

Horsey (D, Ess, Nf, So): Horse island.

Horsforth (YW): Ford that horses can cross.

Horsham (Nf, WS): Enclosure or homestead where horses are kept.

Horsley (common): Horse clearing.

Horstead (K, Nf, WS): Place of horses.

Horton (common): Enclosure or farm in a muddy place.

Horwich (GM): Grey wych-elms.

Hotham (Hm): ?Hood-shaped; ?Place of shelters.

Hothfield (K): Open country with heather.

Hough (common): Grazing enclosure.

Hough (Ch, Db): Hill spur.

Houghton (common): Farm or enclosure on a hill spur (this is the commonest meaning).

Hounslow (Lo): Hund's burial mound.

Housty, Houxty (Nb): Hog sty.

Hove (ES): ?Hood (-shape); ?Shed, shelter.

Hovingham (YN): (Place of) Hofa's people.

Howden (Nb): Hollow valley.

Howe (common): Burial mound.

Howell (L): ?Stream of the cubs.

Hoxton (Lo): Hoc's enclosure or farm.

Hoylake (Mr): Lake in a hollow.

Hoyland (YS): Land by a hill spur.

Hucknall Torkard (Nt): Hucca's valley (the second element is from a Norman family, Torchard).

Huddersfield (YW): Huder's open country.

Huish (D, Do, So, W): Household; Hide, skin (an old English measure of land, 120 acres approximately, considered adequate to maintain a free family – the measure probably varied from one region to another).

Hull (Hm): ?Muddy river. (The town takes its name from the river.)

Hull (common): Hill.

Hulme (common): Small island or water-meadow; Dry land in a fen.

Hulton (La, St): Hill farm or enclosure.

Humber: Meaning is uncertain.

Humberston (Hm): Hunbeorht's stone.

Hungerford (common): Ford leading to infertile land.

Hunger Hill (common): Hunger (implying 'barren') hill.

Hungerton (L, Le): Infertile farm.

Hunmanby (YN): Village of the dog-keepers.

Hunslet (YW): Huna's stream.

Hunstanton (Nf): Huntan's enclosure or farm.

Hunston (Sf): Hunter's farm.

Hunston (WS, Ca): Hun's stone.

Huntingdon (Ca): Huntsman's hill.

Huntington (Ch, H & W, St, YN): Same as **Huntingdon**.

Huntley (Gl, St): Huntsman's wood.

Hunton (Ha): Farm of the hounds.

Hurdlow (Db): Treasure mound.

Hurley (Brk, Wa): Forest in a corner or bend.

Hurn (Do, Ha): Land by a bend.

Hursley

Hursley (Ha, Cu): Horse clearing.
Hurst (common): Wooded hill, hillock, copse.
Hurstpierpoint (ES): Wooded hill of de Pierrepont
 (this last name means 'stone bridge').
Hurworth (Du): Enclosure made from hurdles.
Huthwaite (Nt, YN): Clearing on a spur of land.
Hutton (common): Farm on a hill spur or spur of
 land.
Huyton (La): Enclosure or farm by a landing-place.
Hyde (common): Same meaning as **Huish**.
Hythe (Ess, Ha, K): Landing-place.

Ickenham (Lo): Ticca's village.
Icknield Way (an old set of Saxon roads that went
 from Norfolk to Dorset): 'Icknield' is possibly
 related to the Iceni people.
Ickworth (Sf): Ica's enclosure.
Idle (YW): ?Idle or uncultivated land.
Ightham (K): Ehta's homestead.
Ilam (St): Place at the (river) Hyle (an old Celtic name
 meaning 'slow river').
Ilchester (So): Roman fort on the (river) Yeo (or
 Ivel).
Ilderton (Nb): Alder-tree farm.
Ilford (Lo): Ford across the (river) Hyle (now
 Roding).
Ilfracombe (D): Aelfred's valley.
Ilkeston (Db): Ealac's hill.
Ilkley (YW): Illica's wood or clearing.
Ilminster (So): Minster (church or religious house)
 on the (river) Isle.

Ilsley (Brk): Hild's wood or clearing.

Imber (W): Imma's lake.

Immingham (Hm): Homestead of Imma's people.

Ince (La, Mr): Island, water meadow.

Ingatestone (Ess): At the stone in Ing (?'people of Giga').

Ingham (L, Nf, Sf): ?Inga's homestead; ?Farm on common land; ?River-meadow farm.

Ingleborough (YN): Hill fort.

Ingleby (Db, YN): Village of the Angles.

Inglesham (W): Ingin's homestead or river meadow.

Ingleton (YN): ?Hill farm; ?Ingeld's farm.

Inglewood (Brk): Wood on a hill.

Inglewood (Cu): Wood of the English.

Ingram (Nb): Grassland or pasture farm.

Inham(s) (Ca, L): Land newly taken into cultivation.

Inholms (common): Land newly taken into cultivation.

Inkpen (Brk): Hill.

Innings (K, Hrt): Land newly taken into cultivation.

Inskip (La): Osier basket (for catching fish) island.

Instow (So): (St) John's religious place or church.

Ipplepen (D): Ipela's fold.

Ipswich (Sf): Gip's building.

Ir(e)by (common): Village of the (Scandinavian) Irish.

Irlam (GM): Homestead of the (river) Irwell.

Ironbridge (Sa): Ewe's bridge.

Ir(e)ton (Db, YN): Farm of the (Scandinavian) Irish.

Irthington (Cu): Farm on the (river) Irthing (last name is unexplained).

71

Irthlingborough

Irthlingborough (Nth): Fort of the ploughmen.
Isleworth (Lo): Gislhere's enclosure.
Islington (Lo): Gisla's hill.
Islip (Nth): ?Slope or slippery place.
Iver (Bk): Steep bank.
Ivinghoe (Bk): Spur of land of Ifa's people.
Ivybridge (D): Ivy (-covered) bridge.
Ixworth (Sf): Gicsa's enclosure.

Jarrow (T & W): (Place of) the marsh-dwellers.
Jervaulx (YN): Ure (river) valley.
Jesmond (T & W): The mouth of Ouse Burn.
Johnby (Cu): John's village.

Kearsley (GM): Cress clearing.
Kedleston (Db): Ketel's farm or enclosure.
Keele (St): Cow hill.
Keighley (YW): Cyhha's wood or clearing.
Kellet (La): Slope with a spring.
Kelvedon (Ess): Cynelaf's (a woman's name) valley.
Kempsey (H & W): Cymi's island.
Kempshot (Ha): Kemp corner of land ('kemp' may indicate a plant but the meaning is uncertain).
Kempston (Bd): Farm or enclosure by the (river) bend.
Kempston (Nf): Cymi's enclosure or farm.
Kemsing (K): Cymesa's place.
Kendal (Cu): Valley of the (river) Kent.
Kenley (Lo, Sa): Cena's wood or clearing.
Kenilworth (Wa): Cynehild's (woman's name) farm or enclosure.

Kennet (W): Meaning is uncertain.

Kennington (Brk, Lo): The enclosure of Cena's people.

Kensal Green (Lo): The green of the king's wood.

Kensington (Lo): Cynesige's farm or enclosure.

Kent: ?Land of the Cantii; ?Corner land.

Kenton (Lo): Cena's farm or enclosure.

Kepwick (YN): Marketplace, trading-place or building.

Kersey (Sf): Cress island.

Kerswell (D, H & W): Cress spring.

Kesteven (L): Woodland meeting-place, district with a meeting-place.

Keston (Lo): Cyssi's stone.

Keswick (Cu, Nf, YW): Cheese farm.

Kettering (Nth): Meaning is unexplained.

Kettleby (Db, Le, L): Ketill's village.

Kettlewell (YN): Spring in a narrow valley.

Kew (Lo): Quay by a projecting piece of land.

Keynsham (Av): ?Caegin's homestead; ?Caegin's water-meadow.

Keyworth (Nt): Enclosure of stakes.

Kidbrook(e): Kite brook.

Kidderminster (H & W): Cyda's or Cydela's church or religious house.

Kidlington (O): Enclosure of Cydela's people.

Kilburn (Db, YN): ?Stream alongside a (lime) kiln; ?Cylla's stream.

Kilburn (Lo): ?Royal stream; ?Cattle stream.

Kimberley (Nf, Nt, Wa): Cyneburg's, Cynemaer's, Cynebald's (in order) wood or clearing.

Kimbolton (H & W, Hm): Cynebald's farm or enclosure.

Kingsbridge (D): King's bridge.

Kingsbury (Wa): Cyne's fort.

Kingsbury (Lo): King's manor.

King's Cliffe (Nth): King's sloping place.

Kingsley (Ch, Ha, St): King's wood.

King's Lynn (Nf): King's pool.

Kingsteignton (D): King's farm on the (river) Teign.

Kingston (common): King's farmstead or manor.

Kingswear (D): King's weir.

Kingswood (Av, Gl, Sr, Wa): King's wood.

Kinsbourne (Hrt): Cyne's tumulus or burial-place.

Kippax (YW): Cyppa's (?) ash tree.

Kir(k)by (common): Village with a church, church village.

Kirkgate (common): Church street.

Kirkham (La, YN): Church village.

Kirkhaugh (Nb): Church in an enclosure.

Kirkland (Cu): Church land, land belonging to a church.

Kirkland (La): Grove of trees by a church.

Kirklees (YW): Forest or clearing belonging to a church.

Kirkleatham (Le): Church at the slopes.

Kirkoswald (Cu): Church of Oswald.

Kirton (Hm, L, Nt, Sf): Village with or belonging to a church.

Kitley (D): Kite wood.

Knapton (Le, Nf, H & W, YN): Cnapa's enclosure or farm.

Knaresborough (YN): Cenheard's fort.

Knavenhill (H & W): Cnapa's hill.

Knebworth (Hrt): Cnebba's enclosure.

Knighton (common): Farm of the retainers or young men.

Knightsbridge (Lo): Bridge of the retainers or young men.

Knockholt (Lo): Oak wood.

Knottingley (YW): Wood or clearing of Cnotta's people.

Kno(w)le (common): Hillock, knoll.

Knowsley (GM, Mr): Cenwulf's or Cynewulf's forest or clearing.

Knutsford (Ch): Cnut's ford.

Kyloe (Nb): Cow pasture.

Lacock (W): (Place on) a small stream.

Laindon (Ess): Hill by the (river) Lea.

Laithes (Cu): Corn or barley barns.

Lakenheath (Sf): Landing-place of the people who live at the stream.

Lamas (Nf): Lamb marsh.

Lamberhurst (K): Wooded hill of the lambs.

Lambeth (Lo): Landing-place for lambs.

Lambley (Nb, Nt): Lamb pasture.

Lambourn(e) (Brk, Ess): ?Lamb stream; ?Stream running through clay.

Lambton (Du, T & W): Lamb farm or enclosure.

Lamellan (Co): Church of (St) Maeoleoin (latter name means 'servant of Eoin').

Lamport (common): Long market-place.

Lampton (Lo): Lamb farm or enclosure.
Lancaster (La): Roman fort on the (river) Lune.
Lancing (WS): (Place of) the people of Wlenca.
Landican (Mr): Church of (St) Tecan.
Landkey (D): Church of (St) Cai.
Landwade (Ca): Land ford.
Langar (Nt): Long ridge.
Langbaurgh (Cle, YN): Long mound or hill.
Langdale Pikes (Cu): Long valley of steep slopes.
Langdon (common): Long hill.
Langford (common): Long ford.
Langford (Nt): ?Landa's ford; ?Boundary ford.
Langford (Sr): Long market-place.
Langley (common): Long wood or clearing.
Langport (common): Long market-place.
Langrish (Ha): ?Long place or rushes.
Langsett (YW): Long hillside.
Langsford (D): ?Boundary ford.
Langstrothdale (YN): Valley of the long scrubby marshland.
Langthorn (Lo): High thorn tree.
Langthwaite (Cu, La, YN): Long clearing.
Langtoft (Hm, L): Long toft or homestead.
Langton (common): Long farm or enclosure or village.
Langtree (D, La): Long or tall tree.
Lapford (D): Hlappa's ford.
Lapworth (Wa): Hlappa's enclosure.
Larkhill (C, Ess, H & W, W): Lark hill.
Lashbrook (D): ?Leech stream; ?Bog stream.
Latchford (Ch, O): Ford over a stream.

Latchley (Co): Clearing with a stream.

Latchmere (Sr): Leech pool.

Latchmoor, Latchmore (common): Leech pool.

Latton (Ess, W): Leek enclosure or farm.

Laughton (common): Leek enclosure or farm.

Laughton (L): Enclosed farm.

Launceston (Co): ?Church of (St) Stephen ('ton' was added later).

Launcherley (So): Boundary wood.

Laund(e)s (D, La, Le): Woodland pasture.

Lavenham (Sf): Lafa's homestead.

Laverstock, Laverstoke (Bk, Ha, W): Outlying farm where larks abound.

Layerthorpe (YN): Secondary settlement in a muddy place.

Laytham (Hm): Site of barns.

Lazenby (Cle, YN): Freedman's village.

Lazonby (Cu): Same as **Lazenby**.

Lea (common): Wood or clearing.

Leach (river) (Gl): Stream.

Leadenham (L): ?Leoda's enclosure or farm.

Leake (L, Nt, YN): Brook.

Leam (river) (Wa): ?Elm river.

Leamington (Wa): Farm by the (river) Leam.

Learchild (Nb): Leofric's slope.

Leatherhead (Sr): People's ford.

Leathley (YN): Forest or clearing on the slopes.

Lechlade (Gl): Passage (over Thames) near (river) Leach.

Leckhampstead (Bk, Brk): Leek homestead.

Leckhampton (Gl): Leek village.

Ledbury (H & W): ?Fort at the ridge-slope.
Ledsham (YW): Homestead belonging to Leeds.
Lee (common): Wood or clearing.
Leeds (YW): ?Muddy place; ?Folk dwelling on the (?) boiling river.
Leek (St, Wa): Brook.
Leeming (YN): (Place at the) elm stream.
Leicester: Roman city by the (river) Leire (a Celtic name).
Leigh (common): Wood or clearing.
Leighton (common): Leek enclosure or farm.
Leighton (Nb)) Bright or light-coloured hill.
Leintwardine (H & W): Enclosure on the (river) Lent.
Leith (Sr): Hillside or slope.
Lenacre (Cu): Plot for flax.
Lenham (K): Leana's homestead.
Leominster (H & W): Religious house in the district of Leon.
Lesbury (Nb): Fort of the leech (physician).
Lessness (Lo): Meadow headland.
Letchworth (Hrt): Farm in the enclosed land.
Letcombe (O): Let (?) valley.
Levenshulme (GM): Leofwine's island or water-meadow.
Lever (GM): Place of rushes or flags.
Leverton (Brk, La, L, Nt): Farm where water irises or flags abound.
Lewes (ES): (Place) at the hills.
Lewisham (Lo): Leofsa's homestead.
Lexham (Nf): Homestead of the leech (physician).

Leyburn (K): Lylla's stream.

Leyland (GM, La): Fallow land.

Leyton (Lo): Farm or enclosure on the (river) Lea.

Leytonstone (Lo): Leyton by the stone.

Lichfield (St): ?Open land in the grey forest; ?Grey wood in open country.

Lickpit (Ha): Pit of the corpse.

Lidgate (Co, Sf): Swing-gate.

Lilleshall (Sa): Lill's hill.

Lillington (Do, Wa): Farm or enclosure of Lilla's people.

Limehouse (Lo): Lime-burning oasts or kilns.

Limewood (Nt): ?Heather wood; ?Wood by a hill.

Linacre(s) (Ca, La, Nb): Flax plot or field.

Linch (WS): Ridge, bank.

Linby (Nt): Village with lime trees.

Lincoln: Colony of the hill-fort by a pool.

Lindfield (WS): Open country with lime trees.

Lindhurst (K, Nt): Lime-tree wood.

Lindisfarne (Nb): Island of the Lindisfaran (?Lindsey people).

Lindley (Le, YW): Clearing where flax is grown.

Lindrick (Nt, YN): Lime-tree stream.

Lindridge (H & W, L): Lime-tree ridge.

Lindsey (L): Lindon (Lincoln) island – place takes its name from the main town. ('Lindis', which is the main root, probably means 'island in a lake'.)

Lindsey (Sf): Lelli's island.

Ling (Nf): Heather.

Lingfield (Sr): Open country of the forest-dwellers.

Lingwood (Nt): Wood by a hill.

Link (H & W): ?Side of a hill; ?Cultivated hill-terrace.
Linkenholt (Ha): Wood on the hill.
Linley (Sa): Clearing for flax.
Linslade (Bd): Passage by the hill.
Linthwaite (YW): Flax clearing.
Linton (K): Farm of Lilla's people.
Linton (Nb): Farm on the (river) Lyne.
Linton (common): 'Flax farm' is the most common
    meaning. Sometimes the meaning is 'lime-tree
    farm'.
Lintz (Du): Hill.
Linwood (Ha): Lime-tree wood.
Lipe (So, W): Leap.
Lipgate (ES): Leap-gate (deer but not cattle could
    cross).
Lipyeate (So): Leap-gate (see **Lipgate**).
Liskeard (Co): Fort or court (?of the rock).
Litchardon (D): ?Corpse enclosure (i.e., graveyard);
    ?Hill of the corpses.
Litchborough (Nth): ?Hill with an enclosure;
    ?Corpse hill.
Litlington (Ca): Enclosure of Lytel's people.
Litlington (ES): Little enclosure or farm.
Littleborough (GM, Nt): Little fort.
Littlehampton (WS): Little home farm ('little' is a
    later addition).
Littleport (Ca): Small market or town.
Little Tey (Ess): Little enclosure.
Littleton (common): Small farm or enclosure.
Liverpool (Mr): ?Pool with thick or discoloured
    water.
Liversedge (YW): ?Kind of sedge.

Lizard Point (Co): High fort or court (plus 'point').

Llanymynech (Sa): Church of the monks.

Llanwarne (H & W): Church of the alder trees.

Load (So): Water-course.

Lockwood (YN, YW): Enclosed wood.

Lode (Ca, Gl): Water-course.

Lofthouse (YN, YW): House with a loft or upper floor.

Loftus (Cle): House with a loft or upper floor.

London: Uncertain; probably Celtic name, taken over by the Romans and Latinised. 'Londinium' was the Roman name.

Longford (common): Long ford.

Longleat (W): Long stream.

Longley (H & W, YS, YW): Long forest or clearing.

Long Melford (Sf): Long settlement by the mill ford.

Long Mynd (Sa): Long ridge.

Longridge (La): Long ridge.

Longton (La, St): Long farm or enclosure.

Longtown (Cu): Long farm.

Lonsdale (La, Cu): Lune (river) valley.

Looe (Co) : Inlet, pool.

Loose (K): Pigsty.

Loosley (Bk): Clearing with a pigsty.

Loseley (Sr): Clearing with a pigsty.

Lostwithiel (Co): End part of Withiel (?'upland wood').

Lothersdale (YW): Thieves' valley.

Loud (river) (La): The loud or noisy one.

Loudham (Nt, Sf): Hluda's homestead.

Loughborough (Le): Luhede's fort.

Loughton (Bk, Ess, L): Luca's farm or enclosure.

Lound (common): Grove.
Louth (L): (Place of the) loud river (i.e., river Lud).
Lower Lode (Gl): Lower river-crossing.
Lowestoft (Sf): Hloover's plot of land or homestead.
Loweswater (Cu): ?Leafy lake.
Lowick (Nb): Dairy farm on the (river) Low.
Luccombe (So): Lufa's valley.
Lud (river) (L): Loud (river).
Ludbrooke (D): Loud brook.
Ludford (Sr): Loud ford (i.e., noisy waters or rapids).
Ludgate (Lo): Postern gate.
Ludham (Nf): Luda's homestead.
Ludhill (Hm, YW): Loud (spring) hill.
Ludlow (Sa): Hill or mound by loud waters or rapids.
Ludwell (Db, Nth, O, So, W): Loud spring.
Lugwardine (H & W): Enclosure on the (river) Lugg.
Lullingstone (K): Lulling's farm or enclosure.
Lulworth (Do): Lulla's farm or enclosure.
Lumb (La, YW): Pool.
Lumford (Db): Ford across a pool.
Lumley (Du, YN): Pool wood.
Lund (common): Grove, small wood.
Lundy Island (D): Puffin island.
Lune (river) (La, Cu): ?River; ?Health-giving river.
Lunt (La): Grove, small wood.
Lupton (Cu): Hlupa's farm or enclosure.
Lustleigh (D): Leofgiest's forest or clearing.
Luton (Bd): Enclosure or farm on the (river) Lea.
Lutterworth (Le): Enclosure by the (river) Hlutre.
Lychpole (WS): Pool of the corpse.
Lydbrook (Gl): Loud brook.

Lyd(e) (river) (D, H & W, So): Loud one.

Lydd (K): (Place) on the slopes.

Lyddel Water (Cu): Dale that is loud with rushing water.

Lydford (D): Ford across the (river) Lyd.

Lydiard (So, W): ?Hill, high place.

Lydiate (H & W, La): Swing-gate.

Lydney (Gl): Sailor's island.

Lyme, Lyne (GM, St): ?Elm forest.

Lyme (Do, Ch): Noisy stream, torrent.

Lyminge (K): District around the (river) Limen (?elm river).

Lymington (Ha): Farm or enclosure on the (river) Limen or Lyman.

Lymm (river) (Ch): Noisy stream, torrent.

Lymn (L, La): Place of elms.

Lympne (K): Elm river.

Lympstone (D): Leofwine's farm or enclosure.

Lyndhurst (Ha, K, Nt): Lime-tree wood.

Lyneham (O, W): Flax farm.

Lyn(n) (D, Nf): Pool, lake.

Lynton (D): Farm on the (river) Lyn (river name is Celtic meaning 'lake' or 'river').

Lypiatt (Gl): Leap-gate (allowing deer but not cattle to cross).

Lytham (La): (Place) on the slopes.

Mablethorpe (L): Malbert's outlying farm.

Macclesfield (Ch): ?Macca's or Maccel's open land.

Madeley (H & W, Sa, St): Mada's wood or clearing.

Maghull (Mr): Corner or secluded place where mayweed abounds.

Maidenhead (Brk): Maidens' landing-place.

Maidenwell (Co, L): Maidens' spring.

Maidstone (K): ?Maidens' stone; ?People's stone (marking a meeting-place).

Maidwell (Nf): Maidens' spring.

Makerfield (La): Open land by a wall or ruin.

Malden (Lo): Hill with a cross.

Maldon (Ess): Hill with a cross.

Malham Tarn (YW): Gravelly place at the hill pool.

Malling (K): (Place of) Mealla's people.

Malmesbury (W): Fort of Maol Dubh ('Maol' is 'servant'; 'Dubh' is either 'black' or a personal name).

Malpas (Co): Bad or difficult passage.

Maltby (Cle, L, YN): Malti's village.

Malton (YN): Middle farm or enclosure.

Malvern (H & W): Bald or bare hill.

Mamhead (D): Hill pass.

Manchester: Roman fort of Mamucium (?'breast-shaped hill').

Mangotsfield (Av): Mangod's open country.

Manningham (YW): Settlement of Maegen's people.

Manningtree (Ess): ?Manna's tree; ?Many trees.

Mansergh (Cu): Man's shieling, hill or summer pasture.

Mansfield (Lo): Common field.

Mansfield (Nt): Open land by Mam (a hill – 'mam' is a Celtic word meaning 'mountain pass').

Mapledurham (Ha, O): Maple homestead.

Mappleton (Db, Hm): Maple farm or enclosure.

Mappowder (Do): Maple.

Marazion (Co): Little market.

March (Ca): Boundary.

Marden (K): Woodland pasture for mares.

Marden (ES, WS): Boundary hill.

Maresfield (ES): ?Open country abounding in martens; ?Open country by a marsh.

Marfleet (Hm): Boundary stream.

Margate (K): Gap in the cliffs leading to the sea.

Market Bosworth (Le): Bosworth with a market.

Market Deeping (L): Deep fen market.

Market Lovington (W): The market at the farm of Lava's people.

Market Rasen (L): Market at the plank bridge.

Marlborough (W): ?Maerla's hill; ?Hill of the gentians.

Marley (common): See 'Martley'.

Marlow (Bk): 'Mar' is from 'mere', meaning 'lake'. The other element is obscure, possibly suggesting a remnant of a lake or former lake.

Marple (GM): Hill by the boundary valley.

Marrs (Hm, YS): Marsh.

Marsden (La, YW): Boundary valley, valley with a boundary-mark.

Marsh (common): Marsh, fen.

Marske (Cle): Marshes.

Marston (common): Marsh farm.

Marsworth (Bk): Maessa's enclosure or farm.

Marten, Martin (common): Pool farm.

Mar(t)ley (H & W, YW): Marten wood.

Martock (So): Place by a lake.

Marton (common): Pool farm.

Marylebone (Lo): (St) Mary's brook.

Maryport (Cu): Harbour called after the builder's wife, Mary Senhouse (1760).

Masham (YW): Maessa's homestead.

Massingham (Nf): Settlement of Maessa's people.

Matlock (Db): Oak of the assembly-place.

Maulden (Bd): Hill with a cross.

Mayfair (Lo): Fair held in the month of May.

Mayfield (St, ES): Open country abounding in mayweed.

Meare (So): Lake.

Medbourne (Le, W): Meadow stream.

Medlar (La): Middle shieling or summer pasture.

Medlock (river) (GM): River flowing through meadows.

Medmenham (Bk): Middle river-meadow.

Medway (K): Meaning is uncertain.

Meece (St): Moss, mossy place.

Meesden (Hrt): Mossy hill.

Melbourn (Ca): Stream alongside which milds (various thick-leaved plants) grow.

Melbourne (Db): Mill stream.

Melbourne (Hm): Middle stream.

Meldon (D): Multi-coloured hill.

Meldon (Nb): Hill with a cross.

Melksham (W): Milk (?) meadow.

Mellor (Db, GM, La): Bare or bald hill.

Melmerby (Cu, YN): Melmor's village.

Melplash (Do): Mill pool.

Meltham (YW): ?Mill stream.

Melton (common): Middle farm or enclosure.

Mendip (So): Hill valley.

Menston (YW): The enclosure of Mensa's people.
Meopham (K): Meapa's homestead.
Mere (common): Pool.
Meriden (WM): Pleasant valley.
Merriden (Sr): Pleasant valley.
Mersea (Ess): Sea island.
Mersey (river): Boundary river.
Merske (YN): Marsh.
Merston (common): Marsh farm.
Merton (D, Lo, Nf, O): Pool farm.
Messingham (Hm): Same as **Massingham**.
Methley (YW): Middle island.
Mevagissey (Cu): (Church of) St Mewa and St Ida.
Mexborough (YS): Meoc's fortified place.
Micklethwaite (Cu, YW): Large clearing.
Middleham (Du, YN): Middle homestead.
Middlesbrough (Cle): Middle fort.
Middlesex: (Territory of the) Middle Saxons.
Middleton (common): Middle farm or enclosure.
Middlewich (Ch): Middle building or farmstead.
Midgley (YW): Wood or clearing infested with midges.
Midhurst (WS): Middle wood or wooded hill.
Milbo(u)rne (common): Mill stream.
Mildenhall (Sf, W): Milda's secluded place or corner of land.
Mile end (Ess, Lo): End of the mile (from Colchester and Aldgate respectively).
Milford (common): Mill ford.
Millbrook (Bd, Ha): Mill brook.
Millom (Cu): (Place) at the mills.

Millwall

Millwall (Lo): (River) wall on which mills stand.

Milnrow (GM): Row of houses by a mill.

Milnthorpe (Cu, Nt, YW): Outlying farm or dependent settlement with a mill.

Milton (common): Two different meanings: 1, Middle farm; 2, Mill farm.

Milverton (So, Wa): Farm by the ford with a mill.

Mimms (Hrt, Lo): Meaning is unexplained.

Minchinhampton (Gl): ?Nuns' home farm; ?Nuns' high farm.

Minehead (So): Hill headland.

Minety (W): Mint (the plant) stream.

Minstead (Ha, WS): Mint (the plant) place.

Minting (L): (Place of) Mynta's people.

Mirfield (YW): Pleasant, open country.

Mitcham (Lo): Large homestead.

Mitcheldean (Gl): Large ravine.

Mitchley (Lo): Large wood or clearing.

Mitford (Nb): Ford between (at the confluence of) two streams.

Mitton (La, H & W, YN): Farm or enclosure at the meeting of streams.

Moatlow (common): Moot or meeting hill.

Modbury (D, Do): Moot hill.

Molesey (Sr): Mul's island.

Monkton (common): Two different meanings: 1, Monks' house; 2, Monks' farm (from which monks received revenue).

Montacute (So): Pointed hill.

Moor (common): Two meanings: 1, High, uncultivated land; 2, Marsh land.

Moorgate (Lo): Gate at the marsh or moor.

Morden, Mordon (Ca, Do, Du, Sr): Hill in a marsh.

More (common): Same as **Moor**.

Morecambe (La): ?Great bay; ?Curving inlet.

Moresby (Cu): Maurice's village.

Moreton (common): Farm in a marsh or moor.

Morland (Cu): Moor grove.

Morley (common): Wood in or by a marsh or moor.

Morpeth (Nb): Path of the murder.

Morthoe (D): ?Stump; ?Hill or promontory.

Mortlake (Lo): ?Lake in which young salmon are caught; ?Morta's lake.

Morton (common): Farm in a marsh or moor.

Morwenstow (Co): Church of St Morwenna.

Moseley (St): Moll's wood or clearing.

Moseley (H & W): Forest or clearing with mice.

Moss (YW): Morass, marsh.

Moss Bank (common): Mossy slope.

Mossley (GM): Wood by mossland.

Moss Side (Cu, GM, La, Mr): Edge of the mossland, mossy bank.

Moston (Ch, GM, Sa): Farm in or by a mossland.

Mottisfont (Ha): Spring of the moots or assemblies.

Mottram (GM): Pig farm.

Moulton (common): ?Mula's enclosure or farm; ?Mule farm.

Mount Sorrel (Le, W): 'Mount' is 'hill'. 'Sorrel' is more difficult to explain. The whole name may be an importation of a French placename.

Much Wenlock (Sa): Large (place of the) white monastery.

Murton (common): Farm in a fen or moor.
Musgrave (Cu): Grove with mice.
Muswell (Lo): Mossy spring.
Mutlow (Ch): Mound of the moots or assemblies.
Mytholmes (YW): Confluence of streams.
Mytholmroyd (YW): Clearing at the junction of streams.

Nailsea (Av): Naegl's island.
Nailsworth (Gl): Naegl's enclosure.
Nantwich (Ch): Famous salt-works.
Narborough (Le): Fort at the narrow pass.
Naseby (Nth): Hnaef's village (originally 'fort').
Nash (common): (Place of) ash trees.
Nayland (Sf): River land.
Naze (common): Headland or ridge.
Neasden (Lo): Nose-shaped hill.
Nechells (Sr, St, WM): Land added to a village or reclaimed.
Needham (common): Needy or poor homestead.
Nelson (La): The town took its name from the Lord Nelson Inn, around which it grew up in the 19th century.
Nesbit(t) (Du, Nb): Nose-shaped bend.
Ness (common): Headland or ridge.
Neston (Ch): ?Nose-shaped hill; ?Hill headland.
Neswick (Hm): Dairy farm on a headland.
Netheravon (W): Lower river.
Nethercot(e) (common): Lower cottages.
Netherston (common): Lower farm.
Netley (Sa): Nettle clearing.

Nettlecombe (Do, So, IW): Nettle valley.

Nevedon (Ess): Flat valley.

Newark (Nt. Nth, Sr): New work or building.

Newbiggin (common): New building(s).

Newbold(s) (common): New dwelling(s).

Newbottle(s) (Bk, Nt, T & W): New dwelling(s).

Newbury (Brk, So): New fort or castle.

Newby (common): New settlement or village.

Newcastle (common): New castle.

Newent (Gl): New place.

New(n)ham (common): New homestead or village.

Newhaven (ES): New harbour.

New Haw (Sr): New enclosure.

Newington (common): New farm or enclosure.

Newland(s) (common): Land newly brought into cultivation.

Newmarket (Ca): New market.

Newnham (common): New homestead or village.

Newport (common): New market town.

Newsham (common): New houses.

Newton (common): New farm or enclosure.

Nidd (river) (YW): Bright (water).

Ninebanks (Nb): Nine banks or hills.

Nolton (L): Farm of the wethers.

Norbiton (Lo): Northern outlying grange or (barley) farm.

Norbury (common): Northern fortified place.

Norfolk: Northern people.

Norham (Nb): Northern homestead.

Normanby (YN): Village of the Northmen (Norwegians); see next entry.

Normanton (common): Farm of the Northmen (Northern Vikings from Norway as distinct from the Danes).

Northallerton (YN): Aelfhere's or Aelfred's north farm or enclosure.

Northam (D): Northern farm.

Northam (Ha): Northern river-meadow.

Northampton (Nth): (North) home farm. 'North' was added to distinguish it from Southampton.

Northaw (Hrt): Northern enclosure.

Northenden (GM): Northern enclosure.

North Ferriby (Hm): Northern village at the ferry.

Northleach (Gl): North place on the stream

Northolt (Lo): Northern nook.

North Shields (T & W): (North) shielings.

Northwich (Ch): Salt-works to the north (of Nantwich).

Northumberland: Land (and its dwellers) north of the Humber.

Northwold (Nf): Northern forest.

Norton (common): Northern enclosure or farm.

Norwich (Nf): Northern dwelling or dairy farm.

Norwood (common): Northern wood.

Nosterfield (YN): Open country with a sheep fold.

Nottingham (Nt): Homestead of Snot's people.

Notton (Do, YW, W): ?Farm of the wethers.

Nuneaton (Wa): Nunnery of the farm by the stream.

Nuthurst (La, WS, Wa): Wooded hill where nuts grow.

Nutley (Ess, Ha, ES): Nut wood.

Oadby (Le): Audi's village.

Oakengates (Sa): Oaken gate.

Oakham (Le): Occa's homestead.

Oakhanger (Ch, Ha): Oak wood on a steep hill.

Oakington (Lo): Farm or enclosure belonging to Toca's people.

Oakley (common): Oak wood.

Oakworth (common): Oak enclosure.

Oare (Brk, So, W): Edge of a slope or hillside.

Occold (Sf): Oak wood.

Ockbrook (Db): Oca's brook.

Ockendon (Ess, Lo): Wocca's hill.

Ockham (Sr): Occa's homestead.

Odiham (Ha): Wooded homestead.

Offa's Dyke: (King) Offa's earthwork (fortifications between England and Wales).

Okehampton (D): Farm on the (river) Okement.

Olantigh (K): Small enclosure of the holly trees.

Oldbury (common): Old fort.

Oldham (GM): Old (long-occupied) water meadow or island in a fen.

Oldland (Av): Old land.

Ollerenshaw (Db): Alder copse.

Ollerton (Ch, La, Nt): Alder farm.

Olney (Bk): Olla's island.

Olney (Nth): Lonely clearing.

Ongar (Ess, Ha): Grazing land.

Orchard (Co, D, So): Orchard; apple garden.

Orchardleigh (So): Orchard wood.

Orcheton (D): Apple farm.

Ore (Sf): Same as **Oare**.

Orford (La): Upper ford.

Orford (Sf): Ford at the sea shore.

Ormerod (La): Ormr's clearing.

Orm(e)sby (Cle, L, Nf): Ormr's village.

Ormskirk (La): Ormr's church.

Orpington (Lo): Farm or enclosure of Orped's people.

Orton (common): (Usually) farm or enclosure on a river bank.

Orwell (Hrt): Treasure spring (spring where valuables are thrown in for luck).

Ossett (YW): ?Fold where thrushes abound; ?Osla's sheep-fold.

Osterley (Lo): Clearing with a sheep fold.

Oswaldtwistle (La): Oswald's tongue of land between streams.

Oswestry (Sa): Oswald's tree (i.e., cross).

Otley (Sf, YW): Otta's wood or clearing.

Otmoor (O): Otta's fen.

Otterburn (Nb, YW): Otter stream.

Otterton (D): Farm on the (river) Otter.

Ottery St Mary (D): St Mary's church on the (river) Otter; 'Ottery' is 'otter stream'.

Oulton (Sf, YW): Old farm.

Oulton (Cu): Wulfa's farm or enclosure.

Oundle (Nth): Territory of the Undalas (?) people.

Ouse (river) (Yorks): Water.

Ousterley (Du): Clearing with a sheepfold.

Over (Ca): River bank.

Over (Ch, Db): Slope, ridge.

Overton (common): Farm or enclosure on a river bank or slope.

Ovingham (Nb): Homestead of Ofa's people.

Owlpen (Gl): Olla's pen or small enclosure.

Oxcombe (L): Ox valley.

Oxenhope (YW): Blind valley with oxen.

Oxford (O): Ox ford.

Oxhey (Hrt, H & W): Enclosed pasture for oxen.

Oxley (St): Clearing for oxen.

Oxshott (Sr): Ocga's or Occa's corner of land.

Oxted (Sr): Place where oaks grow.

Oxton (Mr, Nt, YN): Ox farm.

Paddington (Lo): Farm of Padda's people.

Paddock Wood (K): Paddock or small enclosure
with a wood nearby.

Padiham (La): Homestead of Pada's people.

Padstow (Co): Place or church of St Petroc.

Padworth (Brk): Peada's enclosure.

Paignton (D): Paegna's farm or enclosure.

Painswick (Gl): Dairy farm. ('Pain', from Pain
FitzJohn, d. 1137, was added later.)

Pamber (Ha): Meaning is uncertain.

Pangbourne (Brk): Stream of Paega's people.

Panton (L): Farm on a hill.

Parham (Gl, Sf, WS): Pear homestead.

Parkham (D): Small enclosure in a meadow or water-
meadow.

Parr (GM): Enclosure.

Patching (Ess, WS): (Place of) Paecci's people.

Patchway (ES): Paecci's shrine or temple.

Pateley Bridge (YN): Wood or clearing by a path.
('Bridge' was added later.)

Patrington (YE): Meaning is unexplained. It possibly
incorporates 'Patrick', an Irish-Norwegian name.

Patterdale

Patterdale (Cu): Patrick's valley.
Peak Tor (Db): Hill (each element means 'hill').
Peasmarsh (So, Sr, ES): Peas marsh.
Peckham (K, Lo): Enclosure by or on a hill.
Pelton (Du): ?Peola's burial mound.
Pembury (K): ?Fort of Pap's people.
Pendlebury (La): Fort on the hill.
Pendle Hill (La): First part of name also means 'hill'.
Pendleton (La): Farm or enclosure by or on hill.
Penge (Lo): ?Hill wood; ?End of the wood.
Penhill (YN, W): First element also means 'hill'.
Penistone (YS): ?Penny's stone; ?Pening's stone; ?Hill stone or place.
Penkridge (St): Hill (both elements mean 'hill').
Penn (Bk, WM): Hill.
Penn (K): Small enclosure, a pound.
Penning(s) (W): Cattle enclosure.
Pennines: Invented name from 'Apennines'; means heads or hills.
Pennington (Ha, La): Manor for which a penny rent is paid.
Penny Bridge (common): Bridge on which a penny toll is paid.
Pennytoft (L): Manor for which a penny rent is paid.
Penrith (Cu): Hill ford.
Penryn (Co): Promontory, headland.
Penshurst (K): Pefen's wooded hill.
Pensnett (WM): ?Fold on a piece of (wood) land; ?Wood on a hill.
Penwith (Co): Promontory (and an unexplained second element).

Penyghent (YN): ?Head of the open country; ?Boundary district.

Penzance (Co): Holy headland.

Peper Harrow (Sr): Pipera's shrine or temple.

Perranporth (Co): St Piran's port.

Perry (Ca, K, St): Place of pears.

Pershore (H & W): Riverbank abounding in osiers or willows.

Perton (St): Pear farm.

Peterborough (La): Town or borough of (St) Peter (dedication of a monastery).

Peterlee (Du): New town named after Peter Lee (d. 1935), a trade union leader.

Petersfield (Ha): Open country of (St) Peter (a church dedication).

Petherton (So): Enclosure or farm on the (river) Parret.

Pett (K, ES): Hollow, pit.

Petworth (WS): Peota's enclosure or farm.

Pevensey (ES): Pefen's river.

Pewsey (W): Pefe's island.

Pickburn (YS): ?Pike stream; ?Pica's stream.

Pickering (YN): ?(Place of) Picer's people; ?Place of the peak/hill people.

Pickhill (Ess, YN): ?Conical hill; ?Pica's nook.

Pick Hill (K): ?Conical hill.

Pickmere (Ch): Pike pool.

Pickthorne (Sa): Prickly thorn.

Pickworth (Le, L): Pica's enclosure.

Picton (Ch, YN): Pica's farm or enclosure.

Piddle (common): Marshy place, pool.

Piece (common): Small plot of land.

Pigdon (Nb): ?Conical hill; ?Pica's pasture.
Pill (Av): ?Willow.
Pilton (common): Creek or pool farm.
Pinfold (Nb): Pound.
Pinhoe (D): Hill, ridge.
Pinkhurst (Sr, WS): Finch copse.
Pinner (Lo): ?Pinna's slope or riverbank.
Pinnock(s) (Ha, Gl, W): ?Small pen or enclosure; ?Small hill.
Pirbright (Sr): Pear-tree wood.
Pirton (Hrt, H & W): Pear-tree farm.
Pitt (D, Ha): A hollow.
Pla(i)sh (Sa, So): Shallow, marshy pool.
Plaistow (D, Db, K, Lo, WS): Playing ground.
Plashet(t) (Lo, Sr): Place enclosed by interlaced fencing.
Plashford (Co): Ford across a pool.
Plasset (Nf): Enclosure made with interlaced fencing.
Pleck(s) (common): Small plot of land.
Pleshey (Ess): Enclosure with interlaced fencing.
Plessey (Nb): Enclosure with interlaced fencing.
Plot(s) (Nt, YW): Plot of land.
Plumley (Ch): Plum-tree clearing.
Plumpton (common): ?Plum orchard; ?Plum-tree farm.
Plymouth (D): Mouth of the (river) Plym.
Pocklington (Hm): Farm or enclosure of Pocela's people.
Pollard (Hm): Marshy land.
Polperro (Co): 'Pol' is 'port'; the rest is uncertain.
Pontefract (YW): Broken bridge.

Ponteland (Nb): Land on a river.
Pool(e) (common): Pool.
Pooley (Cu): Hill by the pool.
Poplar (Lo): (Place by) the poplars.
Porlock (So): Enclosure by the harbour.
Portbury (Av): Fort by the harbour.
Portgate (Nb): Gateway; Way through the gap (in Hadrian's Wall).
Portishead (Av): Harbour headland or ridge by the harbour.
Portland (Do): Land with harbour, land around the harbour.
Portslade (ES): River-crossing at the harbour.
Portsmouth (Ha): Harbour mouth.
Portway (common): Road to or through a market town.
Potter's Bar (Hrt): Gate kept by a man called Potter.
Poulton (common): Pool farm.
Pound (common): Pound, enclosure for animals.
Poundisford (Co): ?Ford of the overseer of the pound; ?Pinder's ford.
Poundstock (Co): Place with a pound.
Powderham (D): ?Homestead in marshy land; ?Low-lying land reclaimed from the sea.
Prescot(t): (Gl, Mr, O, Sa): Priests' cottage.
Prestbury (Ch, Gl): Priests' manor.
Presteigne (Sa): Community of priests.
Preston (common): Priests' manor or farm.
Prestwich (GM): Priests' dwelling-place or farm.
Prestwick (Nb): Priests' farm.
Prittlewell (Ess): Babbling brook.
Prudhoe (Nb): Pruda's spur of land.

Puckeridge (Hrt): Puck's (a hobgoblin) ridge.
Pucklechurch (Gl): Church of little Puck (hobgoblin).
Puddle (Dock) (Lo, Nf): Puddle or pool (see 'Piddle').
Puddletown (Do): Farm in a marsh.
Pudsey (YW): Pudoc's river land.
Purbeck (Do): ?Bittern headland; ?Bittern beak; ?Ridge frequented by bittern.
Purbrook (Ha): Puck's stream.
Purleigh (Ess): Bittern wood or clearing.
Purley (Lo): Pear-tree wood or clearing.
Purley (Brk): Bittern wood or clearing.
Purton (Gl, St, W): Pear-tree farm.
Pusey (O): Island where peas are grown.
Putley (H & W): Kite (the bird) wood.
Putney (Lo): Putta's landing-place.
Puttenham (Hrt, Sr): Putta's homestead.
Puxton (Av): Pukerel's farm or enclosure.
Pyrton (O): Pear-tree farm.

Quantock (So): Edge, rim.
Quarles (Nf): ?Round place or hill; ?Place by or with (stone) circles.
Quarndon (Db): Quern hill (where millstones are obtained).
Quarrendon (Bk): Same as **Quarndon**.
Quarrington (Du): ?Farm of the millers; ?Quern hill.
Queenborough (K): Queen's fort (Philippa, wife of Edward III).
Queensbury (YW): Literally: Queen's fort. It was given in 1863.
Quinton (Nth, Wa, WM): Queen's manor.
Quorndon (Le): Quern hill.

Radbourne(e) (Db, Wa): Reed stream.

Radcliffe (GM, Le, Lo, Nb, Nt): Red cliff or steep hillside.

Radford (common): Red ford.

Radford (O): Riding ford.

Radipole (Do): Pool abounding in reeds.

Radlett (Hrt): Road junction.

Radley (Brk): Red wood or clearing (probably a reference to soil colour).

Radstock (Av): Place by the road (Fosse Way).

Radwinter (D): ?Middle vineyard.

Radwinter (Ess): ?Raedwynn's (a woman's name) tree.

Rainford (Mr): Regna's ford.

Rainham (Ess, K): (Place of) the Roegingas.

Raise (Cu): Cairn.

Rampside (Cu): Ram's head (a shape).

Ramsbottom (GM): ?Valley bottom of the rams; ?Valley bottom of the wild garlic.

Ramsey (Ca, Ess): Island or riverside land where wild garlic grows.

Ramsgate (K): Hraefn's gap (in the sea cliffs).

Ransworth (Nf): ?Randi's enclosure; ?Enclosure on a border.

Ravenglass (Cu): Glas' share (of land).

Ravenscar (YN): Raven rock or cliff.

Ravenscroft (Ch): ?Hraefn's (personal name?) cottage; ?Raven cottage.

Ravensden (Bd): ?Valley of the ravens; ?Hraefn's valley.

Ravensthorpe (Nth, YN): ?Outlying farm of the ravens; ?Hraefn's outlying farm.

Rawdon (YW): Red hill.

Rawmarsh (YS): Red marsh.

Rawreth (Ess): Heron brook.

Rawtenstall (La): ?Roaring pool; ?Rough-grazing farm.

Ray (river) (W): At the river.

Rayleigh (Ess): ?Roe clearing; ?Rye clearing.

Rayton (Nt): Bailiff's farm.

Rea (river) (C, Sa, Wa): At the river.

Reading (Brk): (Place of) Reada's ('red-haired') people.

Reaveley (Nb): Bailiff's wood or clearing.

Reculver (K): ?Headland.

Redbourn (Hrt, L): Reed stream.

Redcar (Cle, YW): Marsh abounding in reeds.

Redditch (H & W): ?Reed ditch; ?Red ditch.

Rede (K, Sf): Clearing in a wood.

Redhill (Sr): Red slope.

Redmain (Cu): ?Stony ford; ?Red cairn.

Redmire(s) (Du, YN): Swamp abounding in reeds.

Red Pike (Cu): Red, conical hill.

Redruth (Co): Red ford.

Reepham (L, Nf): Bailiff's homestead.

Reeth (YN): Stream.

Reigate (Sr): Roe gate.

Repton (Db): Hill of the Hrype people.

Restormel (Co): Moor of the bare hill.

Retford (Nt): Red ford.

Rhode(s) (GM, YW): Clearing.

Rhydd (H & W): A ford.

Ribble (La, YW): ? Dividing river.

Ribchester (La): Roman fort on the (river) Ribble.

Ribston (YN): The stone of the Hrype people.

Riccall (YN): Tributary (literally, 'calf') of the (river) Rye.

Ricebridge (Sr): Brushwood causeway in a marsh.

Richborough (K): (Roman) fort of Rutupiae (?'muddy creeks').

Richmond (Lo, YN): Strong or fortified mound or hill.

Rickmansworth (Hrt): Ricmaer's enclosure.

Ridge (common): Ridge (originally from the back of a beast).

Ridgebridge (Sr): Bridge or causeway in a marsh.

Ridgeway (common): Unmetalled track that follows ridges across country.

Riding (YN, YS, YW): A third part of the shire.

Ridley (Ch, Nb): Cleared wood place.

Ridley (Ess, K): Wood clearing with reeds.

Rievaulx (YN): Valley of the (river) Rye.

Rigg (common): Ridge.

Rigton (YN, YW): Farm on a ridge.

Ringmer (ES): Round pool.

Ringstead (Do, Nf, Nth): Round place (circular settlement).

Ringwood (Ha): Boundary wood, wood on a boundary.

Ripley (YW): Wood of the Hrype people.

Ripley (Db, Ha, Sr): Wood or clearing in the shape of a strip.

Ripon (YN): (Place of) the Hrype people.

Risborough (Bk): Hill abounding in brushwood.

Rishton (La): Rush farm.

Rishworth (YW): Rush enclosure.

Ris(e)ley (common): Brushwood clearing.

Robertsbridge (ES): Bridge of Robert (de St Martin).

Rochdale (GM): Valley of the (river) Roch (at an earlier period 'ham' was the second element of the name).

Rochester (K): Roman fort – the first element is unexplained.

Rochford (Ess, H & W): Hunting-dog ford.

Rockley (Nt, W): Rook wood.

Rode (Ch): Clearing.

Roecombe (Do): Deer valley.

Roehampton (Lo): Homestead where rooks are numerous.

Rogate (WS): Roe-deer gate.

Roke (Lo): (Place) by the oak tree.

Rolleston(e) (Le, St, W): Hrolf's farm or enclosure.

Rolleston (Nt): Hroaldr's farm or enclosure.

Rolvenden (K): Woodland pasture of Hrothwulf's people.

Romford (Lo): Wide or roomy ford.

Romiley (GM): Wide wood or clearing.

Romney (K): ?Wide river.

Romsey (Ha): Rum's island or river-meadow.

Romsley (Sa, H & W): Wood of wild garlic.

Rookwith (YN): Rook wood.

Ross (Nb): Headland, peninsula.

Ross (H & W): Hill or moor.

Rossendale (La): ?Moor dale.

Rossington (YS): ?Farm or enclosure of the moor-dwellers.

Rosthwaite (Cu): ?Clearing in a moor.

Rothbury (Nb): Hrotha's fort.

Rotherfield (Ha, O, ES): Open country with cattle.

Rotherham (YW): Homestead on the (river) Rother.

Rotherhithe (Lo): Landing-place for cattle.

Rothley (Le, Nb): Clearing in a wood.

Rothwell (L, Nth, YW): Spring or stream in a clearing.

Rottingdean (ES): Valley of Rota's people.

Rougham (Nf, Sf): Rough farm or enclosure.

Roughton (L, Nf, Sa): ?Rye farm; ?Rough farm.

Rowland (Db): Roe-deer wood.

Rowley (common): Rough wood or clearing.

Rowtor (Db): Rough, rocky hill.

Roxton (Bd): Hrokr's farm or enclosure.

Royd(s) (YW): Clearing in a wood.

Roydon (Ess, Nf, Sf): Rye hill.

Royston (Hrt): Cross of Roheis (name of the lady who donated it – 'ton' was added in the 13th century).

Royton (GM): Rye farm or enclosure.

Ruddington (Nt): Farm or enclosure of Rudda's people.

Rudge (common): Ridge.

Rudyard (St): ?Enclosure where rye is grown; ?Pond where rudd are kept.

Rufford (La, Nt): Rough fort.

Rugby (Wa): Hroca's fort.

Rugeley (St): Wood or clearing on a ridge.

Ruislip (Lo): ?Muddy place abounding in rushes; ?Rushy leap.

Runcorn (Ch): Wide bay.

Runnymede (Sr): Island meadow where councils are held.

Runswick (YN): ?Renne's creek.

Rushcliffe (Nt): Brushwood hillside.

Rushett(s) (K, Sr): Place of rushes.

Rushmoor (Ha, Sr): Moor abounding in rushes.

Rusholme (GM): Place of rushes.

Rushton (common): Rush farm or enclosure.

Rushwick (H & W): Place of rushes.

Ruston (Nf): Brushwood farm.

Ruston (**Parva**) (Hm): Hror's farm (the little).

Rutland (Le): Rota's land or estate.

Ruyton (Sa): Rye farm.

Ryde (Sr, IW): Place of a (small) stream.

Rye (H & W, ES): Island place.

Ryhill (Hm, YW): Rye hill.

Ryhope (T & W): Rough or rugged valley.

Ryshworth (YW): Rush enclosure.

Ryton (Gl, Sa, T & W, YN): Rye farm.

Sabden (La, So): Fir-tree valley.

Saddleworth (YW): Enclosure on a saddle-shaped hill.

Saffron Walden (Ess): Valley of the Britons ('Saffron' was added later because it was grown there extensively).

Saham (Nf): Lake farm or enclosure.

Saighton (Chs): Place of sallows.

St Albans (Hrt): Dedication of an abbey.

St Bees (Cu): (Church of) St Bega.

St Briavel's (Co): (Church of) St Briavel.

St Columb Major (Cu): (Church of) St Columba (the larger).
St Helen's (La): (Church of) St Helen.
St Ives (Co, Hm): (Church of) St Ive.
St Just (Co): (Church of) St Just.
St Mawes (Co): (Church of) St Maudez.
St Neot (Co): (Church of) St Neot.
St Neots (Ca): (Church of) St Neot.
Saintoft(s) (YE, YN): Plot of land (with buildings) clearing by burning.
St Osyth (Ess): (Religious foundation) of St Osgyth.
Salcombe (D): Salt valley.
Sale (GM): Place of sallows.
Salford (Bd, GM, H & W): Ford of the sallows.
Salford (O): Salt ford.
Salisbury (W): Salis (?) fort; ?Sarum (?) fort.
Sall (Nf): Sallow wood.
Sallott (Ess): Small building where salt is stored.
Saltash (Co): Salty place of the ash trees.
Saltburn (Cle): Salty stream.
Salterton, Budleigh (D): Buildings for salt-making (in the parish of) Budda's wood or clearing.
Salterton, Woodbury (D): Farm of the salt-workers (in the parish of the) wood fort.
Saltley (WM): Sallow wood.
Saltmarshe (Hm): Salt marsh.
Saltway (Gl, H & W, Sa): Route along which salt was carried.
Sampford (common): Ford with sandy bottom.
Sandbach (Ch): Sandy stream or valley.
Sandford (common): Ford with sandy bottom.
Sandgate (K): Sandy gap in the sea cliffs.

Sandhurst (Brk, Gl, K): Sandy, wooded hill.

Sando(w)n (Brk, Ess, Hrt, Sr): Sandy hill.

Sandown (IW): Sandy homestead.

Sandpit(s) (common): Sand hollow.

Sandridge (D, Hrt, W): Sandy ridge.

Sandringham (Nf): Sandy homestead of Deorsige's people.

Sandwell (GM): Well with sandy bottom.

Sandwich (K): Buildings or market town on sandy soil.

Sandwith (Cu): Sandy ford.

Sandy (Bd): Sandy island.

Sapcote (Le): Sheep cottage.

Sapley (Ca): Fir-tree wood.

Sapperton (Db, Gl, L): Farm of the soap-makers.

Sart(s) (common): Ground newly taken into cultivation.

Sawbridgeworth (Hrt): Saebeorht's enclosure.

Sawley (Db): Sallow hill.

Sawley (YW): Sallow wood.

Sawrey (Cu): Muddy place.

Sawtry (Ca): Landing-place of the salt-sellers.

Saxham (Sf): Homestead of the Saxons.

Saxmundham (Sf): Seaxmund's homestead.

Saxondale (Nt): Valley of the Saxons.

Saxton (Ca, YN): Farm of the Saxons.

Scafell (Cu): Hill with a shieling.

Scalby (Hm, YN): Skalli's village.

Scales (Cu, La, YN): Temporary hut, resting-place for travellers.

Scarborough (YN): ?Skarthi's fort; ?Hill by a pass.

Scargill (Du): Skraki's ravine.

Scarisbrick (La): Skar's slope.

Scaws (Cu): Woods.

Sceugh (Cu): Woods.

Scholes (GM, YS, YW): (Place of) temporary huts.

Scunthorpe (Hm): Skuma's outlying settlement or dependent farm.

Seaford (ES): Ford by the sea.

Seaham (Du): Farm at the sea.

Seahouses (Nb): Homesteads at the sea.

Seamer (YN): Water, lake.

Seasalter (K): Saltworks at the sea.

Seascale (Cu): Hut or temporary dwelling by the sea.

Seathwaite (Cu): Clearing by the lake.

Seaton (common): Farm or enclosure by the sea.

Sedbergh (Cu): Flat-topped hill.

Sedgefield (Du): ?Cedd's or Secg's open country.

Sedgeley (St): ?Secg's wood or clearing; ?Warrior's wood; ?Wood abounding in sedges or rushes.

Sedgemoor (So): Marshland abounding in sedges.

Sedgewick (Cu): Siggi's building.

Sedgewick (ES): Building in a place with sedges.

Sedlescombe (ES): Valley with a dwelling.

Sefton (Mr): Rush farm or enclosure.

Selborne (Ha): Sallow copse with a spring.

Selby (YN): ?Sallow farm; ?Sallow copse.

Selhurst (YN): Sallow wood.

Selly Oak (WM): Sallow wood.

Selsdon (Lo): ?Sallow copse; ?Seli's hill.

Selsey (WS): Seal island.

Selside (Cu, YN): Mountain pasture with sallows, sallow shieling.

Selston (Db, Nt): Sallow farm or enclosure.
Selworthy (So): Sallow enclosure.
Semer (Sf): Water/lake (both elements have the same meaning).
Semerwater (YN): Lake/water (see **Semer**).
Settle (YN): Seat, dwelling.
Sevenoaks (K): Seven oaks.
Severn (river): Meaning is uncertain.
Shadwell (Lo): Shallow spring.
Shaftesbury (Do): Sceaft's fort.
Shakerley (GM): Wood of the robbers.
Shalford (Ess, Sr): Shallow ford.
Shambles (common): Stall (belonging to butchers).
Shanklin (IW): Cup hill.
Shap (Cu): ?Hill; ?Stone circle.
Shapwick (Do, So): Sheep farm.
Shaw (common): Copse, wood.
Sheen (Lo, St): Shelters.
Sheerness (K): Bright headland.
Sheffield (ES, YS): Open land by the (river) Sheaf ('boundary river', dividing Yorkshire from Derbyshire).
Shelf (Db, YW): Shelving (gently sloping) land.
Shelford (Ca, Nt, Wa): Shallow ford.
Shelley (Ess, Sf, YW): Shelving (gently sloping) land.
Shelley (Nb): Clearing with temporary huts.
Shelton (common): Farm on a bank or shelf.
Shenfield (Ess): Beautiful, open country.
Shenington (O): Beautiful hill.
Shenley (Bk, Hrt, WM): Bright wood or clearing.
Shenstone (H & W): Bright stone.

Shepley (YW): Sheep clearing in a wood.

Sheppey (K): Sheep island.

Shepreth (Co): Sheep stream.

Shepshed (Le): ?Sheep hill; ?Sheep's head (place of animal sacrifice).

Shepton (So): Sheep farm.

Shepway (K): Sheep way.

Sherburn, Sherbo(u)rne (common): Clear stream.

Sheriff Hutton (YN): Sheriff's hill spur.

Sheringham (Nf): Homestead of Scira's people.

Sherston (W): Stone on a steep ridge.

Sherwood (Nt): Wood belonging to the shire.

Shevington (GM): Farm by Shevin hill ('Shevin' possibly means 'ridge' or 'hill').

Shields (T & W): (Place of) temporary huts.

Shifnal (Sa): Scuffa's secluded place or corner of land.

Shildon (Du): Hill with a plateau or peak.

Shilton (common): Farm on a shelf or ledge.

Shiplake (O): Sheep brook.

Shipley (common): Sheep clearing.

Shippen (YW): Cowshed.

Shippon (O): Cowshed.

Shipston-on-Stour (Wa): Farm or enclosure at a sheepwash on the (river) Stour.

Shipton (common): Sheep farm or enclosure.

Shipton (YN): Hip farm.

Shirebrook (Db): Clear stream.

Shirley (common): Wood belonging to the shire.

Shirley (Ha): Clearing where the shire meets.

Shoebury (Ess): Protecting fort.

Shopwyke (ES): Sheep farm.

Shoreham (WS): Homestead at a rock or steep slope.

Shortflatt (Nb): Land in selions (narrow cultivated strips).

Shorwell (IW): Hill spring.

Shotton (Du, Nb): Farm or hill of the Scots.

Shrewsbury (Sa): ?Scrobb's fort; ?Fort of the district called 'The Scrub'.

Shrewton (W): Sherriff's manor.

Shropshire: Shire administered from Shrewsbury.

Shroton (Do): Sheriff's manor.

Shrubland (Sf): Brushwood grove.

Shuckburgh (Wa): Earthwork or hill of the demon.

Shugborough (St): Fort or hill of the demon.

Shunner Howe (YN): Look-out hill.

Shuttleworth (GM): Barred or gated enclosure.

Sidcup (Lo): Flat-topped hill.

Side (common): Hillside slope.

Sidmouth (D): Mouth of the (river) Sid (river in a steep valley).

Sidney (Sr): Broad island.

Silchester (Ha): Roman town of the sallows.

Sileby (Le): Sighulf's village.

Silloth (Cu): Barn by the sea.

Silsden (YW): Unknown element, plus 'valley'.

Sissinghurst (K): Wooded hill of Seaxa's people.

Sittingbourne (K): Stream of the Sittingas people ('slope dwellers').

Skeffington (Le): Farm of Sceaft's people.

Skegness (L): Skeggi's headland.

Skell (river) (YW): Loud river.

Skelmanthorpe (YW): Skelmer's outlying farm.

Skelmersdale (La): Skelmer's valley.

Skelton (common): Same as **Shelton**.

Skelwith (Cu): Noisy ford.

Skiddaw (Cu): Craggy hill.

Skipton (YN, YW): Sheep farm.

Skipwith (YN): Sheep wood.

Slack (Cu, Du, YW): Shallow valley.

Slad(e) (common): Valley.

Slaithwaite (YW): Sloe clearing.

Slaughter (Gl): Slough, muddy place.

Slaughter(s) (WS): (Place of) sloe thorns.

Slaughterford (W): Ford by the sloe thorns.

Sleaford (L): Ford over the (river) Slea ('muddy stream').

Sleddale (Cu, YN): Valley.

Sledmere (Hm): Lake in a valley.

Slimbridge (Gl): Causeway or bridge at a muddy place.

Slimford (Co, D): Ford at a muddy place.

Slinford (WS): Fold on a slope.

Sloley (Nf, Wa): Blackthorn wood, sloe clearing.

Slough (Brk, So, WS): Muddy place.

Smeaton (Co, YN, YW): Farm of the smith.

Smethcote (Ha, Sa, St): Smith's cottage.

Smethwick (Ch, WM): Smith's building.

Smite (T & W, Nt, Wa): ?Running brook; ?Dirty brook.

Smithfield (Cu, Lo): Smooth, open country.

Snaith (Hm): Piece of land.

Snap (ES, W): Boggy land.

Snape(s) (common): Boggy land.
Snitterfield (Wa): Open country where snipe abound.
Sodbury (Av): Soppa's fort.
Softley (Du, Nb): Wood or clearing with soft ground.
Soham (Ca, Sf): Homestead by a lake.
Soho (Lo): Named from a traditional hunting-cry.
Solent (Ha): Meaning is unexplained.
Solihull (WM): ?Pigsty hill.
Solinger (Bk): Sallow wood on a hillside.
Sollom (Cu, La): Muddy enclosure.
Solton (K): Muddy farm.
Solway (Cu): Ford marked by a boulder or pillar.
Somborne (Ha): Swine spring.
Somercotes (Db, L): Huts for use in summer.
Somerford (Ch, Do, Gl, St, W): Summer ford (passable in summertime).
Somerset: Dwellers of the summer settlement.
Somerton (L, Nf, O, So): Summer farm.
Sompting (WS): Swamp- or marsh-dwellers.
Sonning (Brk, O): (Place of) Sunna's people.
Sosgill (Cu): Temporary dwellings at a muddy place.
Southall (Lo): Southern nook or recess.
Southam (Gl, Wa): Southern homestead.
Southampton (Ha): (South) farm on river land.
Southcot(t) (common): Southern cottages.
Southend-on-Sea (Ess): Southern end of the town (Prittlewell).
South Ferriby (L): Buildings by the southern ferry.
Southgate (Lo): South gate (of Enfield Chase).
Southminster (Ess): Southern church.

Southover (Do): South of the river bank.

South Shields (T & W): (South) shielings, southern summer pasture.

Southwark (Lo): Southern (defensive) works.

Southwell (Nt): Southern spring.

Southwick (common): Southern buildings or dwellings.

Southwold (Sf): Southern wood.

Sowerby (common): Muddy farm or settlement.

Spalding (L): (Place of) the Spaldingas people ('dwellers near the ditch').

Spalding Moor (Hm): Moor of the Spaldingas people.

Spaldington (Hm): Farm of the Spaldingas people.

Spaldwick (Ca): Buildings or village of the Spaldingas people.

Sparkford (Ha, So): Scrubland ford.

Speke (Mr): Brushwood.

Spell Howe (YE): Speech mound.

Spelthorne (L): Speech thornbush.

Spenborough (YW): Spen's fort.

Spennithorne (YN): Thorn enclosure.

Spennymoor (Du): Enclosed moor, enclosure on a moor.

Spilsby (L): Spillir's village or settlement.

Spit(t)al (common): Hospital (usually attached to a religious house).

Spitalfields (Lo): Hospital fields.

Spital Hill (Nt): Hospital hill.

Spithead (Ha): Headland facing the sandspit.

Spofforth (YN): First element is uncertain: 'forth' means 'ford'.

Springfield (common): Open land with a spring.

Springthorpe (L): Outlying farm or village with a spring.

Spurn Head (Hm): Projecting land.

Stafford (St): Ford by a landing-place.

Staindrop (Du): Valley with stony ground.

Staines (Lo): (Place) at the stone (?Roman milestone).

Stainforth (YN): Stony ford.

Stainland (YW): Stony land.

Stainton (common): Stony farm.

Staithes (YN): Landing-place.

Stalbridge (Do): Bridge built on piles or pillars.

Stalybridge (GM): Bridge by the wood where staves are cut.

Stamford (common): Stony ford (often where a Roman road crossed).

Standish (Gl, GM): Stony pasture.

Standlynch (W): Stony, cultivated terrace.

Stanford (common): Stony ford (often where a Roman road crossed).

Stanground (Ca): Stony ground.

Stanhope (Du): Stony valley.

Stanley (common): Stony wood or clearing.

Stanmore (Ca): Stony lake.

Stannington (Nb): Farm on the paved road (Great North Road).

Stanstead (common): Stony place.

Stanton (common): Stony farm (occasionally a farm near a prominent stone or landmark).

Stanway (Ess, Gl, Sa): Stony road (occasionally a paved Roman road).

Stanwell (Lo, Sr): Stone-lined well.

Stapleford (common): Ford marked by a post.

Stapleton (common): Farm near or with a post or pillar.

Starbeck (YW): Sedge stream.

Stargill (Cu): Ravine abounding in sedge.

Start Point (D): Tail-shaped point of land, promontory.

Statford (St): Horse fold or enclosure.

Statham (Ch): Landing-place.

Stathe (So): Landing-place.

Staunton (common): Same as **Stanton** – farm with stony ground.

Staveley (common): Wood where staves are cut.

Steel (Cu, Nb, YS): Ridge.

Steel (Sa): Stile.

Steep Holme (Av): Steep island.

Steeple Aston (O): Aston with a (church) steeple.

Steeton (YW): Tree-stump farm.

Stepney (Lo): Stybba's landing-place.

Stetchworth (Ca): Tree-stump enclosure.

Stevenage (Hrt): Strong gate.

Stewkley (Bk): Tree-stump clearing.

Stewton (L): Tree-stump farm.

Steyning (WS): (Place of) Stan's people or dwellers at the stone.

Stibbington

Stibbington (Ca): Tree-stump farm, one from which trees have been cleared.

Stickford (L): Ford in a long or narrow island.

Stiffkey (Nf): Tree-stump island.

Stile (Cu): Stile.

Stilton (Ca): ?Farm with a stile.

Stirchley (Sa, WM): Bullock clearing.

Stitches (Ca): Balk or unploughed boundary-strip in a common field.

Stivichall (WM): Corner of land or recess with tree-stumps.

Stockbridge (Do, Ha, WS): Bridge made of tree-stumps, stock bridge.

Stock, Stoke (common): Three main meanings: 1, Place; 2, Monastery; 3, Dependent settlement or farm.

Stocking (common): Two main meanings: 1, Clearing with stumps; 2, Building made of planks.

Stockleigh (common): Two main meanings: 1, Clearing with stumps; 2, Wood belonging to a religious foundation.

Stockley (common): Same as **Stockleigh**.

Stockport (Ch): ?Market at an outlying or dependent place; ?Stock ford.

Stocksbridge (YS): Bridge of tree-stumps.

Stockton, Stoughton (common): Three main meanings: 1, Enclosure with tree-stumps; 2, Farm belonging to a religious house; 3, Farm dwelling made of logs.

Stockwell (common): Two main meanings: 1, Well by or near tree-stumps; 2, Stream with a tree trunk bridge.

Stoke (common): Same as **Stock**.

Stoke Canon (D): Religious place of the Canons Regular.

Stoke Mandeville (Bk): Meeting-place (which came into the possession of the Mandeville family).

Stokenchurch (Bk): Church build of logs, timber church.

Stokesley (YN): ?Forest belonging to a religious foundation.

Stone (common): Stone or stones (the name tends to have different origins).

Stonehenge (W): Hanging-up stones.

Stonehouse (common): House built of stone.

Stoneleigh (Sr, Wa): Stony wood or clearing.

Stone Pike (Cu): Stone, conical hill.

Stone Raise (YN): Stone cairn.

Stonyhurst (La): Stony, wooded hill.

Stotfold (Bd, Du): Fold or enclosure for horses.

Stoughton (common): Same as **Stockton**.

Stourbridge (G, WM): Bridge over the (river) Stour ('strong river').

Stourport (H & W): Port on the (river) Stour.

Stourton (St, W, Wa, YS): Farm or enclosure by the (river) Stour.

Stow(e) (common): Three main meanings: 1, Place; 2, Assembly place; 3, Holy place or monastery.

Stowell (Gl, So, W): ?Stone-lined well; ?Stony spring.

Stowmarket (Sf): Market of the meeting-place.

Stradbroke (Sf): Brook by a (Roman) road.

Strand (D, K, Lo): Riverside way.

Stratford (common): Ford at which a Roman road crosses a river.

Stratton (common): Farm by a Roman road.

Streat, Street (common): (place by) a Roman road.

Streatham (Lo): Homestead by a Roman road.

Strensal (YN): ?Streon's corner of land.

Stretford (common): Same as **Stratford**.

Stretton (common): Same as **Stratton**.

Strickland (Cu): Bullock ('stirk') land.

Strid (YN): ?Place that can be stridden over, a stride; ?Marshy place.

Strood, Stroud (common): Marshy land abounding in brushwood.

Stubbin (Nt, YN): Place of tree-stumps, a clearing.

Stuchbury (Nth): Stut's fort.

Studland (Do): Horse herd land.

Studley (common): Clearing with a horse herd.

Stukeley (Ca): Clearing with stumps.

Stump Cross (common): Cross from which the top or head is gone.

Sturminster (Do): Religious house or church by the (river) Stour.

Sturry (K): Region of the (river) Stour.

Sturton (L, Nb, Nt, YW): Same as **Stratton**.

Stuston (Sf): Stut's farm.

Sudbury (Db, Lo, Sf): Southern fort or manor.

Suffolk: The Southern folk (of the East Angles).

Sugden (Sr): Swamp hill.
Sugden (YW): Swamp valley.
Sugwas (H & W): Sparrow (?) swamp.
Sugworth (Bk): Sucga's enclosure.
Sulgrave (Nth): Valley grove.
Sunbury (Sr): Sunna's fort.
Sunderland (Cu, Du, La, Nb, T & W): Land separated from the main estate.
Sunningdale (Brk): Valley of Sunna's people.
Surbiton (Lo): Southern (barley) farm or outlying grange.
Surrey: Southern district (i.e., in relation to Middlesex).
Sussex: (Place of the) South Saxons.
Sutterby, Sutterton (L): Shoemaker's farm.
Sutton (common): Southern enclosure or farm.
Swadlincote (Db): Svartling's cottage.
Swaffham (La, Nf): Homestead of the Swabian(s).
Swalcliffe (O): Cliff of the swallows.
Swale (Brk, K, YN): Whirling river.
Swallowcliffe (W): Cliff of the swallows.
Swanage (Do): ?Herdsman's dwelling; ?Swannery.
Swanbourne (Bk, WS): Swan stream.
Swancote (Sa): Herdsman's hut.
Swanley (K): ?Swain's (herdsman's) clearing; ?Swan's (a personal name) wood or clearing.
Swanmere (Ha): Swan marsh.
Swanscombe (K): Herdsman's or Swan's (a personal name) enclosure.
Swanton (K, Nf): Herdsman's (swain's) farm.

Swaythling (Ha): Track in a hollow.
Swinbrook (O): Pig brook.
Swinburne (Nb): Pig stream.
Swinden (YN): Pig valley.
Swindon (Gl, St, W): Pig hill.
Swinefleet (Hm): Creek, channel.
Swinehead (Bd, Gl, L, St): Pig head.
Swineshead (Bd, L, YN): Pig's head.
Swinford (common): Pig ford.
Swinscoe (St): Pig wood.
Swinside (Cu): Pig hillside.
Swinton (GM, YN, YS): Pig farm.
Sydenham (Lo): Same as **Chippenham**.
Sydenham (D, O, So): Wide river-meadow.
Syke(s) (Ca, GM, YW): (Place by a) stream.
Syston (Le): ?Sigehaeth's farm or enclosure.

Tadcaster (YN): Tata's Roman fort.
Taddiford (Db): Toad ford.
Tadley (Ha): Toad wood or clearing.
Tamar (river) (Co, D): ?Dark river.
Tame (river) (St, Wa): ?Dark river.
Tamworth (St): Enclosure by the (river) Tame.
Taplow (Bk): Taeppa's tumulus (burial mound).
Tarleton (La): Tharaldr's farm.
Tarn (common): Small lake.
Tarn Flat (La): Flat ground with a lake.
Tarporley (Ch): ?Pear-tree wood by a hill.
Tarrant (river) (Do): ?River liable to flood.
Tattenhall (Ch): Tata's corner of land or secluded spot.

Tattershall (L): Tathere's corner of land.

Taunton (So): Farm or enclosure by the (river) Tone.

Taverham (Nf): ?Farm with red soil.

Tavistock (D): Religious house by the (river) Tavy.

Tawton (D): Farm on the (river) Taw.

Team (river) (Du, T & W): Same as **Tame**.

Tebay (Cu): Tibba's island.

Teddington (Lo): Farm of Tuda's people.

Tees (river) (Cu, Cle): ?Bright, surging.

Teffont (W): Boundary spring.

Teign (river) (D): Stream.

Teignmouth (D): Mouth of the (river) Teign.

Telford (Sa): ?Tila's ford (town named after the engineer, Thomas Telford, 1757 – 1834).

Teme (river) (Sa, H & W): ?Dark river.

Temple (common): Usually a name for a place that belonged to the Knights Templar.

Tenbury (H & W): Fort by the (river) Teme.

Tendring (Ess): Meaning is uncertain.

Tenterden (K): Swine pasture of the men of Thanet.

Tetbury (Gl): Tette's (woman's name) manor or fort.

Tewin (Hrt): ?Place of the god Tiw or Tig; ?Place of the people of Tiwa.

Tewkesbury (Gl): Teodec's fort.

Tey (Ess): Enclosure.

Thame (O): Named from the (river) Thame.

Thame (river) (O): ?Dark river.

Thames (river): ?Dark river.

Thanet (K): ?Fire island, bright island.

Thatcham (Brk): Thatched homestead.

Thaxted (Ess): Place where thatch is got.

Thelwall (Ch): Deep part of river crossed by a plank bridge.

Thetford (Ca, Nf): People's ford, public ford.

Thingwall (Mr): Assembly field.

Thirlmere (Cu): Lake in a hollow.

Thirlspott (Cu): Deep part of the river, giant's hole.

Thirsk (YN): Marsh.

Thornaby (YN): Thormoth's village.

Thornbrough, Thornborough (Nb, YN): ?Stronghold protected with thorns; ?Mound with thorn trees.

Thornbury (Av, D, H & W, YW): ?Stronghold protected with thorns; ?Mound with thorn trees.

Thorne (Co, K, So, YS): Thorn tree.

Thorney (Ca, Lo, Sf, So, WS): Thorn-tree island.

Thornham (K, La, Nf, Sf): Homestead of the thorn trees.

Thornhaven (Ca): Thorn-tree island.

Thornhill (common): Hill of the thorn trees.

Thornhough (Nt): Thorn enclosure.

Thor(n)ley (D, Du, Hrt, IW, Nth): Thorn wood.

Thornthwaite (Cu, YN): Thorn clearing.

Thornton (common): Farm of the thorn trees.

Thorpe: See **Thrup**.

Thrapston (Nth): ?Thrapsta's farm.

Threlfall (La): Clearing of the serfs.

Threlkeld (Cu): Spring of the serfs.

Threshfield (YN): Place where corn is threshed.

Thrift (common): Wood, wooded countryside.

Thrimby (Cu): ?Thryne's village; ?Village of the thorn trees.

Thrup, Thorpe, Throop(e) (common): Outlying farm, hamlet, secondary or derived settlement.

Thunderfield (Sr): Thor's open country.

Thundersley (Ess): Thor's wood or clearing.

Thundridge (Hrt): Thor's ridge.

Thurcroft (YS): Thorolf's cottage.

Thurrock (Ess): ?(Place of) drains.

Thursley (Sr): Thor's wood or clearing.

Thwaite(s) (common): Clearing.

Ticehurst (ES): Wooded hill of the young goats.

Tichborne (Ha): Spring of the kids or young goats.

Tickhill (YS): Tica's hill.

Tideswell (Db): Tidi's stream.

Tidmarsh (Brk): Tida's marsh.

Tidworth (Ha, W): Tuda's enclosure.

Tilbury (Ess): Tila's fort.

Tilehurst (Brk): Wooded hill of the tiles.

Tilford (Sr): ?Tila's ford.

Tillingbourne (Sr): Tilla's spring.

Tillingdown (Sr): Tilli's down or hill.

Tillingham (Ess, ES): (Place of) Tilli's people.

Tillinghurst (ES): Titta's wooded hill.

Tillington (H & W, St): Tylla's or (Tylli's) farm.

Tillington (WS): Farm of Tilla's or Tulla's people.

Tillworth (D): Ella's enclosure.

Tilshead (W): Tidwulf's hide (see **Hide**).

Tilton (Le): Tella's (Tila's or Tulla's) farm.

Tilty (Ess): Tila's small enclosure.

Timberland (L): Small wood or grove used to provide timber.

Timperley (Ch): Wood from which timber is obtained.

Timsbury (Av): Timber grove (where timber was cut).

Timsbury (Ha): Timber fort.

Tingrith (Bd): Stream of the assembly.

Tintagel (Co): Dadgel's fort.

Tipton (D, St, WM): Tibba's farm or enclosure.

Tirley (Gl): Circular wood or clearing.

Tisbury (W): Tysse's fort.

Titchfield (Ha): Open country with kids.

Tiverton (D): Farm or settlement at the two fords.

Toddington (Bd): Hill of Tuda's people.

Toddington (Gl): Farm of Tuda's people.

Todmorden (YW): Totta's boundary valley.

Toft (common): Plot of ground on which a building stands, site of a homestead.

Tollard (Do, W): Hills crossed by valleys.

Tollesbury (Ess): Toll's fort.

Tolleshunt (Ess): Toll's spring.

Tolpuddle (Do): Tola's fen.

Tonbridge (K): Tunna's bridge.

Tong(e) (common): Tongue, river fork, spit of land.

To(o)thill (common): Look-out hill or mound.

Tooting (Lo): ?(Place of) Tota's people.

Topsham (D): Topp's riverside land.

Torbay (D): Bay at the hill.

Torbryan (D): De Brianne's hill.

Torquay (D): Quay by the hill.

Torridge (D): Rough river.

Torrington (D): Enclosure on the (river) Torridge.

Totland (W): Look-out place.

Totnes (D): Tota's headland.

Tottenham (Lo): Totta's homestead.

Tottenham (**Court**) (Lo): Totta's secluded place, corner of land.

Totteridge (Bk, Lo): Tata's ridge.

Tottington, Totton (Ha, L, GM, Nf): Enclosure of Tota's people.

Towcester (Nth): Roman fort on the (river) Tove.

Tower Hamlets (Lo): Small villages belonging to the Tower (of London).

Toxteth (La): Toki's landing place.

Trafford (GM): Road ford (same as **Stretford**).

Tranmere (Mr): Sandbank of the cranes.

Tranmoor (YW): Crane moor.

Tremaine (Co): Hamlet at the stone.

Trenley (K): Round wood or clearing.

Trent (river): ?Trespassing or flooding river.

Trentishoe (D): Round hill.

Tring (Hrt): Slope with trees.

Trough (common): Trough, valley like a trough.

Troutbeck (Cu): Trout stream.

Trowbridge (W): Bridge made of trees or beams.

Trumpington (Ca): Enclosure of Trumpa's people.

Trundle (WS): Circular hill-fort.

Truro (Co): Meaning is uncertain.

Truscott (Co): Scrub cottage.

Trusley (Db): Scrub wood.

Tuddenham (Nf, Sf): Tuda's homestead.

Tuesley (Sr): Tiw's (a war god) wood or clearing.

Tuesnoad (K): Tiw's piece of land or wood.

Tunbridge Wells (K): Spa waters of Tonbridge.

Tunstall (common): Site of a farm or homestead.

Turleigh (W): Round wood.

Turley (YW): Round wood.

Turndenn (K): Round pig-pasture.

Turnham (Green) (Hm, Lo): Homestead by the (river) bend.

Turton (La): Thor's farm or homestead.

Tusmore (O): ?Thunor's (a god) lake; ?Giant's lake.

Tutbury (St): Tutta's or Stut's fort.

Tuxford (Nt): ?Tuki's ford.

Twickenham (Lo): ?Twica's waterside land; ?Meadow at a confluence of streams.

Twiscombe (D): Tiw's (a war god) valley.

Twisell (Nb): Confluence of two streams.

Twistleton (YW): Farm at the confluence of streams.

Twyford (common): Double ford.

Tyburn (river) (Lo): Boundary brook.

Tyldesley (GM): Tiwald's forest or clearing.

Tyne (river): ?Water.

Tynemouth (T & W): Mouth of the (river) Tyne.

Tysoe (Wa): Tiw's (a war god) hill spur.

Uckfield (ES): Ucca's open country.

Uffculme (D): Uffa's valley.

Uffington (Brk, L, O, Sa): Farm or enclosure of Uffa's people.

Ullswater (Cu): Ulfr's lake.

Ulpha (Cu): ?Wolf hill; ?Ulf's burial mound.

Ulverston (La): Wulfhere's or Ulfar's farm.

Union Street (common): Street where the workhouse (union) of a poor law union was.

Upavon (W): Place further upstream.

Uphill (So): Higher ground.

Upholland (La): Higher Holland.

Upminster (Lo): Upper church (i.e., church on higher ground).

Upney (Lo): (Place) on an island.

Upottery (D): Further upstream than Ottery St Mary.

Upper Lode (Gl): Upper river-crossing.

Uppingham (Le): Village of the dwellers on the hill.

Upton (common): Higher farm or village.

Urmston (GM): Urm's farm or enclosure.

Urpeth (Du): Ox path.

Urswick (La): Village by the ox lake.

Ushaw (Du): Wolves' copse.

Uttlesford (Ess): Wittuc's or Udel's ford.

Uttoxeter (St): Wittuc's heathery place.

Uxbridge (Lo): Bridge of the Wixan people.

Uxendon (Lo): Hill of the Wixan people.

Vange (Ess): Fen district.

Vauxhall (Lo): Hall or manor of Falkes (de Breauté).

Ventnor (IW): (Place of the) Vintener (an officer who commanded 20 men).

Vinegarth (Hm): Vine enclosure.

Waddington (Lo): Wheat hill.

Waddon (Do, Lo): Woad hill.

Wade (Sf): Ford.

Wadebridge (Co): Bridge over a ford.

Waden (**Hill**) (W): Shrine (hill).

Wainfleet (L): Creek or stream fordable by a wagon.

Wainlode (Gl): Wagon river-crossing.

Waitby (Cu): Wet farm or homestead.

Wakefield (Nth, YW): Open country where the wake or festival is held.

Walbrook (Lo): Stream of the Welsh.

Walburn (YN): Spring of the Welsh.

Walcot(t), Walcote (common): Cottages of the serfs or Welsh.

Walden (Ess, Hrt, YN): Valley of the serfs or Welsh.

Wales (So, YS): (Place of) the Welsh.

Walgrave (Nth): ?Grove belonging to Wold (a place now called 'Old').

Wall (Sa): Spring.

Wall (Nb, St): (Roman) wall.

Wallasey (Ch): Island of the Welsh.

Wallingford (Brk): Ford of Wealh's people.

Wallington (common): Farm of the serfs or Welsh.

Wallsend (T & W): End of the (Roman) wall.

Walmer (K, La): Pool of the serfs or Welsh.

Walney (Cu): ?Island of the quicksands.

Walpole (Nb): Pool by the (Roman) wall.

Walpole (Sf): Pool of the Welsh.

Walsall (St): Walh's corner of land.

Walsham (Nf, Sf): Wael's or Walh's homestead.

Walsingham (Nf): Homestead of Waels's people.

Walsoken (Nf): The marsh by the wall.

Waltham (common): Wood homestead.

Walthamstow (Lo): Wilcume's religious house.

Walton (common): Three main meanings: 1, Wood farm (Bk, Ca, Gl, Le, L, Nf, Nth, O, Sa, So, Wa); 2, Farm of the serfs or Welsh (Ch, Db, Ess, K, La, Le, Mr, Sf, Sr, St, YW); 3, Farm by a wall (Cu, Nf, Sr).

Walworth (Du, Lo): Enclosure or farm of the serfs or Welsh.

Wandsworth (Lo): Waendel's enclosure or farm.

Wangford (Sf): Ford by the open fields.

Wansbeck (Nb): ?Bridge crossed by wagons; ?Brushwood causeway.

Wansdyke (Av, Ha, W): ?Woden's dyke.

Wanstead (Lo): ?Place by a small hill.

Wantage (O): (Stream) that dries up.

Wapping (Lo): (Place of) Waeppa's people.

Warboys (Ca): Beacon bush.

Warden (Bd, Du, K, Nb): Watch hill, look-out hill.

Wardington (O): Meaning is uncertain.

Wardle (Ch, GM): Look-out hill.

Wardlow (Db): Look-out hill.

Wardour (W): Watch slope.

Ware (Hrt): Weir.

Wareham (Do): Homestead by a weir.

Wargrave (Brk): Grove by the weirs.

Wark (Nb): Fortification.

Warkworth (Nb): Werca's enclosure.

Warley (Ess): Wood or clearing that had been subject to an agreement.

Warley (Sa): Clearing for pasturing beasts of burden.

Warminster (W): Religious building on the (river) Were.

Warrington (Ch): Enclosure or farm at a weir.

Warsop (Nt): Waer's valley.

Warter (Hm): Felon cross (gallows).

Warton (La, Nb, St, Wa): Enclosure or farm by an embankment or wharf.

Warwick (Wa, Cu): Dwellings by a weir or river dam.

Wasdale (Cu): Lake valley.

Wash (Hm): An estuary that is fordable (water washing across intermittently).

Washbourne (Gl): Wet place.

Washington (T & W): Wassa's farm or enclosure.

Washington (WS): Settlement of the Wassa people.

Watchet (So): Lower wood.

Watendlath (Cu): Hill at the end of the lake.

Waterbeach (Ca): Stream.

Watercombe (Do): Water valley.

Waterfall (St): Swallow-hole, (i.e., place where water goes underground).

Water Lane (common): Lane leading down to a river or watery place.

Watervale (D): Waterfall.

Watford (Hrt): Hunting ford.

Wath (Cu, YN, YS): Ford.

Watling Street: Roman road in the place of the Waeclingas (old name for St Albans).

Watlington (Nf, O): Enclosure of Waecel's (Wacol's) people.

Watton (Hrt): Woad farm (i.e., farm where woad grows).

Watton (Nf): Wada's farm or enclosure.

Watton (YS): ?Wet farm; ?Wet hill.

Waveney (Sf): ?River running through marshy land.

Waverley (Sr): Wood by marshy ground.

Wavertree (Mr): Swaying tree (?isolated young tree).

Weald (common): Forest, woodland.

Wealden (ES): Wood hill.

Wealdstone (Lo): Woodland stone.

Wednesbury (WM): Woden's fort.

Wednesfield (WM): Woden's open country.

Weedon (Bd, Nth): Hill of the shrine or pagan temple.

Weedslade (Nb): Withy (willow) valley.

Weeford (St): Ford by a shrine or temple.

Week(e) (Co, Ha, IW, So): Building(s), habitation(s), dairy farm.

Weeley (Ess): Woodland shrine or temple.

Weeting (Nf): Wet place.

Weeton (Hm, La, YN): Willow enclosure or farm.

Weetwood (Nb, YW): Wet wood.

Weighton (Hm): Enclosure with buildings, dwellings; Enclosure or farm near a village.

Welbeck (Nt): Stream.

Welford (Brk): Willow ford.

Welford (Nth): Ford over the stream.

Well (Ha, K, L, YN): Well, spring.

Welland (H & W): White spring.

Wellesbourne (Wa): ?Corpse stream; ?Stream of the Welsh.

Wellingborough (Nth): Waendel's fort.

Wellington (H & W, Sa, So): Enclosure of the dwellers of the temple wood.

Wellow (Av, Ha, IW, Nt): Spring.

Wells (Nf, So): Springs.

Wellsborough (Le): Curved hill.

Welton (Cu, L, Nth, Hm): Spring farm.

Welwyn (Hrt): (Place of) willows.

Wem (Sa): Marsh.

Wembley (Lo): Wemba's clearing or forest.

Wendover (Bk): White water or stream.

Wenlock (Sa): White monastery.

Wennington (Lo): Farm or enclosure of Wynna's people.

Wensley (Db): Woden's clearing.

Wensley (YN): Waendel's forest or clearing.

Wenslow (Db): Woden's barrow or earthworks.

Wensum (river): The winding one.

Weobley (H & W): Wiobba's forest or clearing.

Weoley (WM): Woodland spring.

Wessex: (Place of) the West Saxons.

West Bridgford (Nt): West bridge over a ford.

Westbury (common): Western fort.

West Camel (So): ?Western border; ?Western, bare hill.

Westcot(t)e (common): Western cottage(s).

Westerham (K): Western homestead.

Westerfield (common): Field(s) on the west side of town; also, western open country.

Westgate (Du, Nb): West gate.

Westham (Do, So, ES): Western homestead.

West Ham (Lo): Western section of the river-meadow.

Westminster (Lo): Western religious house.

Westmorland: Land of the west moor-dwellers.

Weston (common): Western farm or enclosure.

Westward Ho (D): Named from Charles Kingsley's book of that title.

Wetherall (Cu): ?Corner of land; ?River-meadow of the rams.

Wetherby (YW): Farm of the wethers (castrated rams).

Wetherley (Ca): Wood-grazing for wethers.

Wetton (St): Wet hill.

Wetwang (Hm): Wet field.

Wey (river) (Do, Sr): ?Running water.

Weybridge (Sr): Bridge on the (river) Wey.

Weyhill (Ha): Hill of the shrines or temples.

Weymouth (Do): Mouth of the (river) Wey.

Whaddon (Bk, Ca, Gl): Wheat hill.

Whaplode (L): Burbot stream.

Wharfe (river) (YW): Winding river.

Wharles (La): Hill with (ancient) circular earthworks.

Wharton (L): Farm or enclosure from which a watch is kept for attackers.

Wharton (La): Farm of the swaying trees.

Wharton (H & W): Farm near an embarkment or wharf.

Whatborough (Le): Wheat hill.

Wheatacre (Nf): Plot of land where wheat is grown.

Wheathampstead (Hrt): Homestead where wheat is grown.

Wheathill (Sa, So): Wheat hill, hill on which wheat is grown.

Wheatley (common): Clearing where wheat is grown.

Wheldale (YN): Curving valley – like a wheel.

Wheelton (La): ?Ring village; ?Settlement on a round hill.

Wheldale (YW): Curved valley.

Whelpley (Bk, W): ?Clearing or wood of the fox cubs or puppies; ?Hwelp's wood or clearing.

Whernside (YN): Hillside from which millstones are quarried.

Wherstead (Sf): Embankment or wharf.

Wherwell (Ha): Well or spring in a hollow.

Whetstone (Le, Lo): Whetstone (place where obtained).

Whichford (Wa): Ford of the Hwicca people.

Whicham (Cu): Settlement of Hwita's people.

Whickham (T & W): Homestead enclosed by a quickset hedge.

Whielden (Bk): Curved valley.

Whilborough (D): Round hill.

Whilton (Nth): ?Ring village; ?Settlement on a round hill.

Whimple (D): White pool.

Whinfell (Cu): Mountain abounding in gorse or whin.

Whipsnade (Bd): ?Wibba's piece of ground; ?Wibba's wood.

Whissonsett (Nf): Ford of the Wicingas.

Whitburn (T & W): ?White or clear stream; ?Hwita's tumulus; ?Hwita's barn.

Whitby (Ch): ?White village.

Whitby (YN): ?White village; ?Hviti's farm or settlement.

Whitchurch (common): White church (built in bright stone, such as limestone).

Whitcomb(e) (common): Three main meanings:
1, Wide valley; 2, Willow valley; 3, White valley.

Whiteacre (K): Plot of land where wheat is grown.

Whiteborough (Nt): Hill where wheat is grown.

Whitefield(s) (common): Open country with light-coloured soil.

Whitehaven (Cu): Harbour of the white headland.

Whiteway (D, Do, Gl): A way or road of white appearance (as one going through chalk or limestone).

Whit(e)well (common): White or clear well or spring.

Whitley, Whitleigh (common): Clearing with white or light-coloured soil.

Whitney (H & W): At the white island.

Whitstable (K): White pillar where councillors meet (a hundred moot).

Whittingham (La): Homestead of Hwita's people.

Whittington (common): Two main meanings:
1, White farm or enclosure; 2, Hwita's farm or enclosure.

Whittlesey (Ca): Wittel's island.

Whitton (common): Same as **Whittington**.

Whitwell (common): White stream.

Whitworth (La): ?White farm; ?Hwita's farm.

Whorlton (Cu, Nb, YN): ?Ring village; ?Settlement in a round place.

Wibtoft (Wa): Vibbe's plot of land with buildings.

Wichenford (W): ?Ford in the land of the Hwicce people; ?Ford in the wych-elms.

Wichnor (St): Riverbank in the land of the Hwicce people.

Wick (common): Buildings, dwellings.

Wicken (Ca, Ess, Nth): (Place) at the dwellings, dairy farm.

Wickenby (L): Village of the Vikings.

Wickford (Ess): ?Ford by a wych-elm; ?Ford by a settlement.

Wickham (common): ?Dairy-farm homestead; ?Homestead by a Roman settlement.

Wickwar (Gl): Dairy farm (later belonging to the Warre family).

Widcombe (Av, D): Wide valley.

Widecombe, Widdicombe (D): Willow valley.

Widford (Ess, Hrt, O): ?Wide ford; ?Willow ford.

Widnes (La): Wide headland.

Wigan (GM): ?Wigan's place; ?Red place.

Wiganthorpe (YN): Small or outlying settlement of the Vikings.

Wiggenhall (Nf): Wicga's corner of land.

Wiggington (Hrt, Nt, O, YN, Sa): ?Wicga's enclosure or farm.

Wight, Isle of: ?Island; ?Water parting.

Wigmore (H & W): ?Wicga's moor; ?Great wood.

Wigston Magna (Le): Viking farm ('magna' means 'big place').

Wigston Parva (Le): ?Vicg's stone; ?Rocking stone ('parva' means 'small place').

Wigtoft (L): Plot of ground with a dwelling.

Wigton (Cu): Wicga's enclosure or farm.

Wigwell (Db): Wicga's spring.

Wike (YW): Dwelling, dairy farm.

Wilburton (Ca): Wilburg's (a woman's name) farm by the fort.

Wilby (Nf, Nth, Sf): Village of the willows.

Willaston (Ch): Wiglaf's enclosure or farm.

Willenhall (WM): Willow nook.

Willesden (Lo): Hill with a spring.

Willey (Ch, Sa, Wa): Willow wood.

Willingham (Ca, L): Homestead of Wifel's people.

Willingham (Ca, L, Sf): Homestead of Willa's people.

Willington (Bd, Db): Willow farm.

Willington (Du): Enclosure of Wifel's people.

Willitoft (Hm): Willow place, buildings among the willows.

Williton (So): Farm on the (river) Willett.

Willoughby (common): Willow farm, village by the willows.

Wilmington (D): Farm or enclosure of Wilhelm's people.

Wilmslow (Ch): Wighelm's or Wilhelm's burial mound.

Wilsden (YW): Valley of Wilsige's people.

Wilsford (L, W): Wifel's ford.

Wilsthorpe (Db, Hm, L): Wifel's outlying farm.

Wilton (Ca, Cle, Cu, So): Spring farm.

Wilton (W): Enclosure or farm on the (river) Wiley.

Wiltshire: Shire administered from Wilton.

Wimbledon (Lo): ?Winebeald's hill; ?Wynman's hill.

Wimborne (Do): Stream running through pasture land.

Wincanton (So): Enclosure or farm by the (river) Wincawel.

139

Winchcombe (Gl, K): Corner or nook in a valley.

Winchelsea (ES): Island at a bend (in the river Brede).

Winchester (Ha): Roman fort of Venta. ('Venta Belgarum' is 'market of the Belgae', a group of peoples).

Winder (La, Cu): Windy hillside, shieling or wind-shelter.

Windermere (Cu): Vinand's lake.

Win(d)sor (Brk, Do, Ha, Hm, Mr, Sf): Riverbank with a winch for winding boats.

Winestead (Hm): Wife's (a man's name) place or building.

Wing (Ca): Field.

Wingate(s) (GM, H & W, Nb): Pass or gap through which the wind sweeps.

Wingfield (Bd, Db, Sf, W): Open pasture land.

Wingham (K): Homestead of Wiga's people.

Winnats (Db): Pass or gap through which the wind sweeps.

Winnow (Cu): ?High strip of pasture land.

Windscales (Cu): Windy (temporary) huts (shelter against the wind).

Winsford (Ch, So): Wine's (a personal name) ford.

Winskill (Cu): Windy huts or shelters.

Winslow (Bk): Wine's burial mound.

Winster (Db): Wine's thorn bush.

Winston (Du): Wine's farm or enclosure.

Winston (IW): Winsige's farm or enclosure.

Winterbo(u)rne (common): Spring or stream flowing in winter.

Winterton (Hm): ?Farm of Winter's or Wintra's people; ?Farm used in winter.

Wirksworth (Db): Weorc's or Wyrc's enclosure or farm.

Wirral (Mr): Corner of land where bog myrtle grows.

Wisbech (Ca): Valley of the swampy river.

Wisborough (WS): Meaning is uncertain.

Wishford (W): Ford of the wych-elms.

Witchampton (Do): Farm of the dwellers in the settlement.

Witchingham (Nf): Homestead of the Wicingas.

Witham (Ess): ?Wita's homestead; ?Homestead of the councillor.

Witheridge (D): Willow ridge.

Withernsea (Hm): ?Thorn-tree pool.

Withington (Ch, GM, H & W, Sa): Willow-copse farm.

Withycombe (D, So): Willow valley.

Withypool (So): Willow pool.

Witney (O): Witta's island.

Witton (common): Enclosure with buildings or dwellings.

Witton (Nb, Nf, YN): Wood farm.

Wiveliscombe (So): Wifel's valley.

Wivenhoe (Ess): Wifa's ridge or spur of land.

Wo(o)burn (Bd, Bk, Sr): Crooked or winding stream.

Wokefield (Brk): Wocca's open country.

Woking (Sr): (Place of) Wocca's people.

Wokingham (Brk): Homestead of Wocca's people.

Woldale (YW): Wooded valley.

Wolds (The) (Hm, L, Le, Nth): High forest land (eventually deforested).

Wolsingham (Du): Homestead of Wulfsige's people.

Wolstanton (St): Wulfstan's enclosure or farm.

Wolston (Wa): Wulfric's enclosure or farm.

Wolverhampton (WM): Wulfrun's (woman's name) enclosure or farm.

Wolverton (Bk): Wulfweard's farm or enclosure.

Wolvey (Hm, Wa): Enclosure for flocks against wolves.

Wombourn (St): Winding stream.

Wombwell (YW): ?Spring in a hollow; ?Wamba's spring.

Womersley (YS): ?Willow lake.

Woodbridge (Do, Sf): Wooden bridge.

Woodborough (Nt): Fort in or by a wood.

Woodborough (W): Wooded hill.

Woodbury (common): Fort in or by a wood.

Woodchurch (K, Mr): Wooden church.

Woodcote, Woodcot(t) (common): Wooden cottage(s); Cottage(s) in or alongside a wood.

Woodford (common): Ford by or in a wood.

Woodgarston (Ha): Paddock in or beside a wood.

Woodhall (common): Wooden manor house or manor house by a wood.

Woodhay (Brk, Ha): ?Wood enclosed for hunting; ?Enclosure in a wood.

Woodhouse(s) (common): Wooden house(s); House(s) in or by a wood.

Woodlands (Lo): Cultivated land by a wood.

Woodleigh (D, Gl): Clearing in a wood.

Woodley(s) (Brk, Gl, GM, O): Clearing in a wood.

Woodmancote, Woodmancott (common): Woodman's cottage.

Woodmansterne (Sr): Thorn tree by the boundary of the wood.

Woodridings (Lo): Clearing in a wood.

Woodrow (Do, H & W, YW): Lane through a wood.

Woodroyd (YW): Clearing in a wood.

Woodside (common): Wood on a slope; Slope by a wood; Place by a wood.

Woodspring (Av): Wood-grouse copse.

Woodstock (O): Place in a wood.

Woofferton (Sa): Wulfhere's enclosure or farm.

Wookey (So): Noose, snare.

Wool (Do): Well, spring, stream.

Woolacombe (D): Spring in a valley.

Wooler (Nb): Stream bank.

Woolley (Brk, Ca, Co, Gl, Lo, W, YW): Wolf forest.

Woolmer (Hrt): Wolf (-frequented) lake.

Woolpit (common): Pit for trapping wolves.

Woolwich (Lo): Wool (-producing) farm.

Wo(o)tton (common): Farm in or by a wood.

Worcester (H & W): Roman fort of the Wigoran.

Worgret (Do): Felon cross (gallows).

Workington (Cu): Weorc's or Wyrc's farm.

Worksop (Nt): Wyrc's or Weorc's valley.

Worle (Av): Wood, grouse wood.

Worley (H & W): Clearing for oxen or draught animals.

Wormshill (K): Woden's hill.

Wormwood Scrubs (Lo): Rough woodland abounding in reptiles.

Worsbrough (YS): Wyrc's fort.

Worsley (GM): Weorcgyth's forest or clearing.

Worth (common): An enclosed place.

Worthen (Sa): An enclosed place.

Worthing (WS): (Place of) Wurth's people.

Worthy (common): An enclosed place.

Wortley (YS): Wryca's wood or clearing.

Wragby (L, YW): Wraghi's village.

Wragholme (L): Island of the wolves or outcasts.

Wrantage (So): Pasture land for stallions.

Wratting (Ca, Sf): Place abounding in crosswort.

Wraxall (Do, So, W): Corner of land frequented by buzzards.

Wrekin (Sa): Originally 'Viriconium' ('Viriconos's town').

Wrentham (Sf): ?Wrenta's homestead.

Writtle (Ess): Babbling stream.

Wrose (YW): Broken or twisted hill.

Wrotham (K): Wrota's homestead.

Wroughton (W): ?Farm on the winding river.

Wroxall (Wa, W): Corner of the buzzards.

Wroxeter (Sa): Roman city of Viriconium (Viriconos's town).

Wroxham (Nf): Homestead where buzzards abound.

Wroxton (O): Stone where buzzards are found.

Wrythe (Lo): (Place by) a small stream.

Wychaven (H & W): River of the Hwicce people.

Wychwood (O): Wood of the Hwicce people.

Wycombe (Bk): ?Enclosure with buildings.

Wye (K): Pagan temple or shrine.

Wyville (L): Spring of the pagan temple or shrine.
Wyfold (Bk, O): Shrine enclosure.
Wyham (L): Place by the shrines.
Wyke (Do, Sr, YW, W): Same as **Week(e)**.
Wymondham (Le, Nf): Wiemund's homestead.
Wyre (H & W): Forest of the Weogoran people.
Wyton (Hm): ?Farm belonging to a wife; ?Willow farm.
Wyton (Ca): Dwelling-place, farm near a village.

Yapton (WS): Farm or enclosure of Eabba's people.
Yardley (common): Wood from which spars are obtained.
Yarlside (La): The jarl's (nobleman of Scandinavian origin) shieling or hillside.
Yarm (Cle): (Place) beside the fish dams.
Yarmouth (Nf): Mouth of the (river) Yare.
Yarmouth (Nf, IW): ?Gravelly river-mouth.
Yarnfield (So, St, W): Open country where eagles are found.
Yar Tor (D): Rocky hill of the harts.
Yate (Av): Gate.
Yateley (Ha): Gate or gap by a clearing or wood.
Yatesbury (W): ?Geat's fort; ?Fort near a gap.
Yatton (Av, H & W, W): Farm near a gap in the hills, farm in a pass.
Yaxley (Ca, Nf, Sf): Wood of the cuckoos.
Yeading (Lo): (Place of) Geddi's people.
Yeadon (YW): High, hilly ground.
Yealmpton (D): Farm on the (river) Yealm.
Yelverton (D, Nf): Geldfrith's farm.
Yeo (river) (D, So): River, stream.

Yew Bank (Cu): Slope of a hill on which yew trees
  grow.
Yiewsley (Lo): Wife's (a man's name) clearing or
  wood.
York (YN): Evolved from Latin 'Eburacum'
  (probably 'Eburos's place' or 'place of yew trees').
Youlgreave (Db): Yellow grove.
Yoxford (Sf): Oxford.

Zeal(s) (D, W): Place of sallows.
Zennor (Co): (Church) of St Senara.

Some Elements
in English Placenames

ABBREVIATIONS

CE: Celtic
ME: Middle English
OD: Old Danish

OE: Old English
OF: Old French
ON: Old Norse

Ack-, ake-, oak- -ock: Oak tree (Acton, Akeley,
Oakhanger, Matlock): *āc* (OE).

Al- alder-, all-: Alder tree (Alford, Aldershaw,
Allerton): *alor* (OE).

Ap-, apper-, apple-: Apple (Apley, Apperley,
Appleby): *aeppel* (OE).

Arne-, ern(e)-, -arne: House, storehouse (Arne,
Crewkerne, Cowarne): *aern* (OE).

Ash-, esh-, -ash: Ash tree (Ashby, Esholt,
Borrowash): *aesc, esc* (OE).

Avon-, aven-, -avon: River (Avon, Avenbury,
Upavon): *afon* (CE).

Bank, -bank: Bank, hillside, ridge (Bank, Firbank):
banke (OD, ME).

Bar-, be(e)r-, ber, -berrow: Grove, wood (Barrow,
Beer, Adber, Sedge berrow): *bearu* (OE).

Bar-, ber—: Barley (Barton, Berwick): *bere, baer*
(OE).

Bar(k)-, berk-, birk-: Birch tree (Barkham, Berkley,
Birkenhead): *beorc* (OE).

Bar(row)-, berg-, -ber, -bergh, -borough, -burgh:
Hill, mound, tumulus (Barrow, Bergholt,
Farnborough, Whinburgh): *beorg* (OE), *berg*
(ON).

Batch-, beach-, bec-, -bach, -bech, -beach: Stream, valley (Batchcott, Beachampton, Beccles, Sandbach, Wisbech, Waterbeach): *bece, baece* (OE).

Bec(k)-, -beck: Brook, beck, stream (Beckermonds, Birbeck): *bekkr* (ON).

Beech-, bitch-: Beech tree (Beech, Bitchfield): *bēce* (OE).

Bent-: Bent grass, ground covered with coarse grass (Bentley): *bēonet* (OE).

Biggin(g)-, -biggin: Building, house (Biggin, Newbiggin): *bigging* (ME).

Bold-, boot(le), -bold, -bottle: Dwelling, palace (Bold, Bootle, Newbold, Harbottle): *bold, bōtl* (OE).

Booth-, bow-, -bo(o)th: Temporary shelter, herdsman's shelter (Boothby, Bowerdale): *bōth* (OD).

Botham-, bottom-, -bottom: Valley bottom, wide shallow valley (Bothamsall, Bottom, Ramsbottom): *botm* (OE), *botn* (ON).

Brac(k)-: Bracken (Brackenthwaite): *braken* (ME), *brakni* (ON).

Brad, broad-: Broad, wide (Bradford, Broadstairs): *brād* (OE).

Bram-, brim-, bro(o)m-: Broom (Bramley, Bromfield): *brōm* (OE).

Brear-, brere-, brier-: Briar, briars (Brearton, Brereton, Brierley): *brēr* (OE).

Bridge-, brig-, -bridge, -brig(gs): Bridge (Bridgenorth, Brighouse, Tonbridge, Westbriggs): *brycg* (OE).

Brook(e)-, broc(k)-, brough-, -brook, -broke: Stream, water-meadow (Brook, Brockton, Broughton, Ashbrook, Bolinbroke) *brōc* (OE).

Brough-, bur(g)-, -borough, -brough, -bury: Fort, fortified place, manor-house (Brougham, Burgate, Scarborough, Cornbrough, Bloomsbury): *burg, burh* (OE).

Burn-, bourne, brun-, -burn, -bo(u)rne: Stream (Burnby, Bourn, Brunton, Kilburn, Lambourne): *burna* (OE).

Butter-, bitter-: Butter (Butterworth, Bitterley): *butere* (OE).

-by: Farmstead, village (Whitby): *bȳ* (ON).

Cal(d)-, cauld-, chal-, col(d)-: Cold, exposed (Caldecote, Cauldwell, Chalk Farm, Coldcoats): *cald, ceald* (OE).

Camp-, -combe: Enclosed land, field (Campden, Ruscombe, Addiscombe): *camp, comp* (OE).

Carl-, charl-, chorl-: Free peasant, freeman of a lower social order, churl (Carlton, Charlton, Chorlton): *karl* (ON), *ceorl* (OE).

Car(r)-, crick-: Rock, hill (Carham, Cricklewood): *carr* (CE).

Chester-, -caster, -cester, -chester, -xeter: Roman town, fortified camp (Chesterton, Lancaster, Alcester, Manchester, Wroxeter): *ceaster* (OE – from Latin 'castra', a camp).

Church-, cheri-, chir-, -church: Church (Churchill, Cheriton, Chirton, Hornchurch) *cirice* (OE).

Cle(e)ve-, clif(f)(e)-, clive-, -cliff(e)-, -ley: Steep hillside, bank, cliff (Cleveland, Cliffe, Cliveden, Radcliff, Catsley): *clif* (OE).

Clough-, clo-, -cleugh, -clough: Narrow valley, ravine (Cloughton, Clopton, Catcleugh): *clōh* (OE).

Co(a)te-, cottam-, cot(t)on, cote-, -cot(e), - cott: Cottage, shelter (Coates, Cottam, Cotton,

Woodcote, Westcott): *cot* (OE).

Cran-, cor(n)-: Crane (Cranleigh, Cornbrook): *cran* (OE).

Creech-, crich-, crew-: Hill, round hill, barrow (Creech, Crichel, Crewkerne): *crūc* (CE).

Croft-, -croft: Piece of enclosed land, small enclosure (with a building, especially in the North) (Croft, Holcroft): *croft* (OE).

Cros(s)-, -cross: Cross (Crosland, Shawcross): *cros* (ME).

Dal(e)-, -dale: Dale, valley (Dale, Oxendale): *dael* (OE), *dalr* (ON).

Dean(e)-, den(e)- dun-, -den, -don: Valley (Deanham, Denham, Dunsford, Hebden, Croydon): *denu* (OE).

Ditch-, dit-, dish-, -ditch, -dish, -dyke: Ditch, dyke (Ditchford, Ditton, Diss, Shoreditch, Reddish, Wansdyke): *dic* (OE).

Dow(n)-, den-, don-, dun-, -den, -do(w)n, -ton: Hill, down, undulating chalk uplands (Downs, Denham, Donhead, Dunham, Malden, Ashdown, Quarrington): *dūn* (OE).

E-, ea-, ey-, -ey, -y: Stream, river (Eton, Eamont, Eyton, Mersey, Ottery): *ēa* (OE).

E-, ea-, ey-, -ea, -ey, -y: Island, land by water (Eyam, Eathorpe, Eyton, Battersea, Dorney, Caldy): *ēg* (OE).

East-, as-, ast-: East, eastern (Eastoft, Ascot, Aston): *ēast* (OE).

Edge-, -edge, -age: Ridge, edge (Edgeworth, Hathersage): *ecg* (OE).

Ery-, arr-, ark-, -ark(e), -er, -ergh: Shieling, temporary dwelling, shelter (Eryholme, Arram,

Arkholme, Anglezark, Winder, Mansergh): *erg* (ON).

Fel, -field: Open country (in forested area) (Feltham, Huddersfield): *feld* (OE).

Hal-, Haugh-, -hal(l), -al(l): Nook, corner of land, recessed place (Halton, Houghton, Eccleshall, Odsal): *halh* (OE).

Hay, haugh-, haw-, -(h)augh, -hay, -hey: Enclosure, fenced enclosure (Haywood, Haugh, Haw, Bylaugh, Woodhay, Oxhey): *haga* (OE): *hagi* (ON).

Hay-, -hay-, -hey-: Enclosed piece of land, fenced land (Hayes, Harthay, Haringey): *(ge) haeg* (OE).

Head-, -he(a)d, -ide: Head, headland, (end of a) ridge (Head, Gateshead, Hartside): *hēafod* (OE).

Heath-, had-, hat-, hed-, -heath: (Heathfield, Hadleigh, Hatfield, Hedley, Blackheath): *haeth* (OE).

Hill, hil-, hul(l)-, -hill, -el(l), -al(l): Hill, rising ground (Hill, Hilton, Hulton, Churchill, Crichel, Coughall): *hyll* (OE).

Hoe-, hoo-, hu-, -hoe, -o(e): Tongue of high land, ridge, low spur (How, Hoo, Hutton, Wivenhoe, Aynho): *hōh* (OE).

Hol(e)-, holl-, -hae, -al(l), -hole: Hollow, hole (Holbrook, Holloway, Brockhall, Foxholes): *holh* (OE), *hol, hilr* (ON).

Holm(e)-, hulme-, -holm(e), -ham: Water-meadow, island, dry ground in marsh (Holme, Hulme, Axholme, Durham): *holmi, holmr* (ON).

Holt-, -holt, -old: Wood, thicket (Holt, Knockholt, Occold): *holt* (OE).

Hop-, hope-, -(h)op(e), -op, -up: Small valley, blind valley, dry land in a fen (Hopton, Hope, Stanhope,

Alsop, Bacup): *hop* (OE).

How(e)-, (h)oe(e): Hill, (burial) mound, heap
(Howe, Clitheroe): *haugr* (ON).

Hows-, hus-, -house, -us: Dwelling (Howsham,
Husthwaite, Stonehouse, Loftus): *hūs* (OE), *hús*
(ON).

Hurst-, hirst-, her-, -hurst: Small hill, wooded hill
(Hurst, Hirst, Herstmonceux, Sandhurst): *hyrst*
(OE).

Ing(s)-, -ing(s): Meadow, common pasture (Ingham,
Hallings): *eng* (OE).

Kel(d)-, -keld: Spring (Kellet, Threlkeld): *kelda*
(ON).

Kir(k)-, -kerk-: Church (Kirkby, Ormskirk): *kirkja*
(ON).

Lac-, lake-, -lake, -lock: Stream, watercourse
(Ladock, Lake, Mortlake, Medlock): *lacu* (OE).

Land-, -land: Estate, region, soil (Land, Sunderland):
land (OE).

Lang-, long-: Long, extensive, high (Langton,
Longford): *lang* (OE).

Lea-, lee, leigh-, ley(s)-, -ley, -leigh: Wood, clearing,
meadow (Lea, Lee, Leigh, Bingley, Hadleigh): *lēah*
(OE).

Lin(ch)-, leng-, -linch, -lynch, -lin: Ridge, bank
(Linch, Lingwood, Barlinch, Standynch,
Shanklin): *hlinc* (OE).

Lin(d)-, lyn(d)-: Lime tree (Linwood, Lyndhurst):
lind (OE).

Lock-, -lock: Enclosure (Lockwood, Porlock): *loca*
(OE).

Lode-, load-, -lade, -lo(a)d, -lode: Road, path,
watercourse, open drain in fens (Lode, Load,

Cricklade, Abloads, Whaplode): *(ge) lad* (OE).

-low: Low hill, barrow (Harlow): *hlaw, hlaew* (OE).

Lund-, lound-, l(o)unt-, -land: Grove, copse (Lund, Lound, Swanland): *lundr* (ON).

Marsh-, mars-, mers-, -marsh, -mas: Marsh (Marsh, Marston, Merske, Tidmarsh, Lamas): *mersc* (OE).

Mil(l)-, miln-, mel-, -mill: Mill (Milton, Milnthorpe, Melplash, Westmill): *myln* (OE).

Minster-, -minster: Church, religious establishment (Minster, Westminster): *mynster* (OE).

Mont-, -mond, -mont: Hill, mound (Montacute, Richmond, Beaumont): *mont* (OF, ME).

Mo(o)r(e)-, more-, mur-, moor, -more: Moor, fen, wasteland (Morton, Moor, Murton, Dartmoor): *mōr* (OE).

Nas(s)-, naze-, nes-, -nes(s): Headland, projecting ridge (Nassington, Naze, Neswick, Totnes, Lessness): *naess* (OE), *ness* (ON).

Nor(th), -north: North (Norwood, Bridgenorth): *north* (OE).

O(a)re-, or-, -or(e): Border, bank (Oare, Orton, Eastnor): *ōra* (OE).

Over-, or-, -or, -over: River bank, slope (Over, Orton, Eastnor, Ashover): *ofer* (OE).

Per-, pir-, pur-: Pear tree (Perry, Pirbright, Purley): *pyrige* (OE).

Pen(n)-, pin-: Hill, hilltop (Penrith, Pingoe): *pen* (CE & OE).

Po(o)l-, p(o)ul-, -pol(e), -pool, -ple: Pool, stream (Poole, Poulton, Walpole, Liverpool, Cople): *pōl* (OE).

Por(t)-, por-, -port: Harbour, town (Portsmouth,

Porlock, Newport); *port* (OE).

Rad-, red-, rat-: Red (Radford, Redhill, Ratcliffe); *réad* (OE).

Rise-, ris-, rus-: Brushwood (Riseholme, Risborough, Ruston): *hrīs* (OE), *hrís* (ON).

Rish-, ru(i)s-, rysh-, -rish: Rush, rushes (Rishton, Ruislip, Ryshworth, Langrish): *risc* (OE).

Ro(w)-, rough-, ru(f)-: Rough, uncultivated (Rowley, Roughton, Rufford): *rūh* (OE).

Royd-, r(h)ode-, rod-, -rod, -royd: Clearing in a wood, land cleared of trees (Royd, Rode, Ormerod, Holroyd): *rod* (OE).

Ryde-, rye, reth-, -rith, -red: Small stream (Ryde, Rye, Shepreth, Tingrith, Hendred): *rith* (OE).

Sal(e)-, saw-, sel-: Sallow tree (Salford, Sawley, Selbourne): *salh, sealh* (OE).

Sam-, san(d)-, -sand(s): Sand, sandy place or shore (Sampford, Sandford, Cockersand): *sand* (OE).

Scale-, scholes-, -skill, -(s)gill(s), -scales: Hut, temporary dwelling (Scales, Scholes, Winskill, Sosgill, Windscales): *skáli* (ON).

Sea-, sa-, so-, -sea: Sea, lake, marsh (Seahouses, Saham, Soham, Hornsea): *sae* (OE), *saer* (ON).

Shaw-, -shaw: Copse, small wood (Shawbury, Bradshaw): *scaga, sceaga* (OE).

She(e)p-, shib-, ship-, skip-: Sheep (Shepton, Shipley, Skipton): *scēap, scīp* (OE).

Shel(f)-: Shelving land, rock, river (Shelton): *scelf, scylf* (OE).

Side-, syde-, -side, -cett, -sett: Hillside, slope (Side, Syde, Woodside, Fawcett, Langsett): *sīde* (OE). Or shieling, hill pasture: *saetr* (ON).

Slade-, sled-, -slade: Valley (Slade, Sleddale, Greenslade): *slaed* (OE).

South-, sud-, sut-: South, southern (Southall, Sudbury, Sutton): *sūth* (OE).

Sta(i)n-, stam-, ston-, -ston(e), -ton: Stone (Stanley, Stamford, Stonyhurst, Maidstone, Keston): *stān* (OE), *steinn* (ON).

-Stead, -sted (e): Place, dwelling site, site (Elmstead, Felsted): *stede* (OE).

Stock-, stoke-, -stock, -stoke: Religious foundation, (secondary) settlement (Stockton, Stokesley, Tavistock, Basingstoke): *stoc* (OE).

Stow(e)-, -stow(e): Place, religious foundation, assembly place (Stow, Plaistow): *stōw* (OE).

Strat-, stre(a)t-: Roman road, street (Stratford, Streatham, Stretford): *straet* (OE).

Thor(n)-, -thorn(e): Thorn bush, thorn tree, hawthorn (Thornton, Langthorn): *thorn* (OE).

Thorp(e)-, thrup(p)-, -thorp(e): Secondary settlement, hamlet (Thorpe, Thrupp, Layerthorpe): *thorp* (OD), *throp* (OE).

Thwaite-, -thwaite: Clearing, meadow (Thwaite, Micklethwaite): *thveit* (ON).

Toft-, -toft: Homestead, dwelling site, (Toft, Lowestoft): *topt*, *toft* (ON).

-ton: Enclosure, farm village, estate, manor (Felton): *tun* (OE).

Tor-, -ter: Rock, rocky hill (Torbryan, Dunster): *torr* (OE), *tor* (OE).

Wal(l)-: Briton(s), Celtic groups, Welsh, serf(s) (Walcot, Wallasey): *walh*, *wealh* (OE).

W(e)ald-, wal(t)-, wold-, -wold(s): Woodland, high forest land, open upland (denuded of trees) (Weald, Walgrave, Wolds, Northwold): *wald*, *weald* (OE).

Wick-, wig-, week(e), wyke, -wich, -wick: Farm
dairy farm, dwelling, salt-works (Wick, Wyke,
Wigtoft, Week, Droitwich, Chiswick): *wīc* (OE).

Wil(l)-, willough-, wel(l)-: Willow tree (Wilby,
Willoughby, Welford): *wilig, weilig* (OE).

With(y)-, wid-, weet(h)-, -with: Willow tree,
especially osier willows (Withycombe, Widford,
Weeton, Askwith): *withig* (OE).

Wood-, woot-, -wood: Wood, woodland
(Woodside, Wooton, Norwood): *wudu* (OE).

Worth-, -worth Enclosure, homestead (Worth,
Edgeworth): *worth* (OE).